ing style, and a highly individual and "natural" treatment of harmonic rules (parallel fifths and octaves in abundance).

By the end of the eighteenth century, the minister who fought almost exclusively for music educational reforms had been replaced by the local or itinerant musician, choirmaster, precentor, or composer. The rational, epigrammatic and terse language of the Age of Reason differs from the more relaxed, subjective and emotional language of the new craftsman-composer. By the later eighteenth century the various composers were no longer tied to a particular church. Such men as James Lyon, Josiah Flagg, Elias Mann, Andrew Law, and Samuel Holyoke worked in connection with the Presbyterian, Episcopal, and Congregational churches in New England.

Hood, as we see, handles the history of music in New England as the interaction of religion and music. He says:

The history of music in New England, for the first two centuries, is the history of Psalmody alone; and this is so intimately connected with the history of the church, that he who would fully know the one, must understand the other. Between music and religion, in the churches of our land, there has ever been a beautiful and intimate connection. Like the wheels in Ezekel's vision of the cherubim, "when they stood, these stood; and when they were lifted up, these lifted

> up themselves also." As religion waned amid the prosperity and specious errors of a growing country, so music was neglected; and as it revived, the voice of song was renewed. They have ever been reciprocating friends. Music has lent her aid, and religion has sanctified her services.[24]

Himself a representative of this alliance between music and religion, Hood deals with the interaction of theologians, ministers, composers, and congregations within the larger context of American church history.

Protestant church music changed in the course of two centuries because of the interaction of ministers and worshipers. The first change in the basic goals and ideals of the Puritan church came in the period after 1620. The Congregational church was then characterized by a stress on the propriety of praising God through the singing of psalms. Ironically, the strongly exclusive nature of this psalm-singing helped widen a cultural gap between the group which adhered to a mean singing of a few recognized psalm tunes and the group which favored a more plentiful selection of highly embellished and altered tunes, between the group which read music and sang it faithfully as it was written and the group which did not know how to read and rejoiced in altering the tunes according to need and desire, between the persons who owned psalm books and those who did not, between city and

[24] Hood, *A History of Music in New England,* p. 9.

country dwellers. The result was a polarization and a division of forces. In light of the success of tune books (as listed by Hood in his section on the history of books chronologically arranged), it becomes clear that there was a basic change in the role of church music: while the music of the seventeenth-century Puritans was expository, eighteenth-century American Protestant music was more interpretative. The result was the creation of more expressive and individualistic church music. The expressive quality of church music is evident in New England in the fuguing style of writing. Its lack of harmonic activity, especially the absence of dominant seventh chord movements, must be understood, from Hood's view, as a lack of expressive activity. Consequently the Hood who desires expressive activity, harmonies which spring not from formal rule, but rather from nature, is something of an anomaly to the Hood who eloquently pleads for the "reasonableness" of music in an ordered cosmos.

Johannes Riedel

A

HISTORY OF MUSIC

IN

NEW ENGLAND:

WITH

BIOGRAPHICAL SKETCHES

OF

REFORMERS AND PSALMISTS.

———————

By GEORGE HOOD

———————

BOSTON:

WILKINS, CARTER & CO.

1846.

BOSTON:

PRINTED BY FREEMAN AND BOLLES,
DEVONSHIRE STREET.

PREFACE.

EVERY one desires to know something of the history of the art or science in which he is interested. Divest architecture, or any one branch of the natural sciences of its history, and you take away the prime part of all that can interest. So music, if you leave its history unwritten and unread, becomes the mere plaything of the present, instead of the dignified and venerated subject that has been favored by princes and sages, Christians and prophets, ever since the world began.

It was this idea that prompted the writer to collect and arrange the materials for the following pages. His success in finding historical matter has far exceeded his anticipations ; and that which he supposed would end with the scanty materials for a single lecture, has, by much labor, increased to a volume.

This book pretends only to be a history of psalmody, and to extend from the settlement of New England to the beginning of the present century.

In preparing this work, it has been the writer's constant aim, to give the facts as he found them; and if they seem broken or isolated, it must be remembered that, with such material, it was scarcely possible to make a full and consecutive history. The matter has been gathered by much labor, time and expense from different parts of the Union, and frequently in very small portions. The labor has been almost incredible. To show something of its difficulty, there are six consecutive lines that were unfinished more than one year; and the matter of which was gathered at more different times and places, than the number of lines, twice told. But with all its difficulties, the reader may rely upon the truth of the work. It must not, however, be expected that such a production should be entirely free from error; yet all who know its difficulties, will acknowledge its fidelity. Had the materials all been written, though scattered in different libraries, much of the present labor would have been saved; and were all the matter that has been written still in existence, the history would be far from meagre;

or, could that now wasting on dusty shelves, or stowed away in garrets, as useless and cumbersome lumber, be brought out, much useful information on this interesting subject might yet be obtained.

From the old controversial writers, the author has copied freely, preferring their own words to convey information, concerning the subjects upon which they wrote. When a quotation has been made from any book, the authority has been given ; but not always in that which was verbal or written, and not printed. For the latter kind of information, the writer acknowledges his obligation to the late and lamented Mr. Holden, of Charlestown, Judge Mitchell, of Boston, and Rev. Dr. Pierce, of Brookline, Mass. ; to the Massachusetts Historical Society, and the Boston Athenæum, for the free use of their invaluable libraries ; and also to those persons who have so politely furnished materials for the biographical sketches of their friends.

In the department of biography, information was obtained in part from books, and in part from correspondence and conversation with individuals. The information concerning the earlier biographies was obtained mostly from the writings of Cotton Mather, D. D., and from Allen's and Elliot's Biographical Dictionaries.

The writer fondly hopes that this subject will

not be deemed unworthy of attention. All things must have their beginning; and this, though small, is important. We know that our music was mean; but as we hope not to have a low seat among the nations, and as we hope in future to have a history of the art worth preserving, we would not lose the past, but gather it carefully up, and set it with the future, that the contrast may appear the more bright and beautiful. If the music was mean we must not deem it unworthy of notice; and if the composers were ignorant, we must not judge them by our standard of right. They had not the means of studying the science critically, as we have, and the people for whom they wrote were far from being fastidious. But they lived and labored honorably, though in ignorance, and we should respect their intentions.

Believing that he has done what he could for the advancement of music, and for the encouragement of the church, the author presents this work to the musical world, as a veritable history of their art, and to the christian community, as a work that bears upon its pages no small share of the history of the church. It will illustrate the fact, that there has been no great revival of religion, without a corresponding interest in the improvement of music; and no great improvement in music without an increase of religion. If, in this work he has awakened inquiry, by giving interesting facts to the musical world, or words of encouragement to the church, he will esteem it his greatest possible success, and his very ample reward.

PHILADELPHIA, January 1st, 1846.

A HISTORY OF MUSIC
IN NEW ENGLAND

SERIES IN AMERICAN STUDIES

Editor-in-Chief: Joseph J. Kwiat
PROGRAM IN AMERICAN STUDIES
UNIVERSITY OF MINNESOTA

A HISTORY OF MUSIC
IN NEW ENGLAND

WITH BIOGRAPHICAL SKETCHES
OF REFORMERS AND PSALMISTS

By GEORGE HOOD

With a New Introduction by
JOHANNES RIEDEL
PROFESSOR OF MUSIC
UNIVERSITY OF MINNESOTA

JOHNSON REPRINT CORPORATION

New York and London

1970

The edition reproduced here was originally published in 1846

ML
200
. H77

Library of Congress Catalog Card Number:
76-107854

INTRODUCTION

Each musical epoch is usually followed by a period in which a lack of regard for the former's values and aims is manifested. However, this historical myopia becomes, after a reasonable insulation of time, a self-correcting phenomenon. It is, therefore, not surprising to see, after fifty years neglect, the increasing evidence of the nineteenth century being rediscovered by the twentieth. Many twentieth-century works on American music are, for example, now utilizing the information found in George Hood's charming *A History of Music in New England*. The use of this source is in fact a recognition of the value and significance of nineteenth-century American work.

Hood's volume was important throughout the nineteenth century and its value is once more being recognized. The article on psalmody in John W. Moore's *Complete Encyclopedia of Music* (1854)[1] draws a great deal of material from this precious "pocketbook" of "musical puritania." An essay by J. Vila Blake, "Yankee Church Music," in *The Radical* (1870),[2] quotes amply from Hood without giving him credit. There are the brief references to specific items of the Hood work: materials taken from his discussion of the lining-out practice of the Puritans in Henry Wilder

[1] John W. Moore, *Complete Encyclopedia of Music* (Boston: Oliver Ditson, 1854), pp. 752 ff.

[2] J. Vila Blake, "Yankee Church Music," *The Radical,* VII (1870), pp. 494–497.

Foote's *Three Centuries of American Hymnody* (1940), his elaborations to the Ainsworth psalter in Louis C. Elson's *The National Music of America and its Sources* (1899), material from his list of books as used by the early settlers in Henry M. Brooks' *Olden-Time Music* (1888). The examples drawn from Hood by Allen P. Britton in his University of Michigan dissertation, *Theoretical Introductions in American Tune-Books to 1800* (1949), give credit to the diversity and wealth of material which can be found in Hood. They suggest a great deal of unresearched material of seventeenth-, eighteenth-, and nineteenth-century American church music yet to be investigated. Ralph Daniel in his *The Anthem in New England before 1800* (1966) shows a great sense of respect for Hood by having the idea of his book parallel Hood's work.

The substratum of thought from which Hood's book emerges is a curious blend of eighteenth-century rationalism and nineteenth-century transcendentalism. Hood is both a product of eighteenth century rationalism and a participant in the idealistic "genteel tradition" of the nineteenth century. Thus Hood embraces both the rational order of the past and the subjectivism of his own age, with its assertion of the individual's unique relationship to his God. This subjectivism contains in embryo the mortal challenge to the rational order. Hood zealously embraced these conflicting views and their champions in his volume.

A glance at the format of the book will help us understand why a contemporary critic asserted that this volume is "unskilfully, . . . put together." The book is organized into the following seemingly unrelated four sections: (1) "History of Music in New England" (pp. 9–153); (2) "History of Books," chronologically arranged (pp. 154–178); (3) "Origin of Choirs" (pp. 179–201); (4) "Biographical Sketches" (pp. 202–250). These four sections are enclosed by four testimonials (by Judge Nahum Mitchell, Lowell Mason, George J. Webb, A. N. Johnson), Hood's short Preface, and a general index at the end of the tome. The first section, a book in itself, covers "the history of music in New England, for the first two centuries . . . the history of Psalmody alone . . . ,"[3] from the Ainsworth psalter to the "Reformation" (1720–1740). The second section, organized into two parts, is in actuality an annotated bibliography of works from 1741 to 1799. Its first part (1741–1770) contains a few "choice gleanings" from miscellaneous items such as Benjamin Franklin's publication of Watts' Hymns (1741) with a letter from Watts to Cotton Mather concerning this publication (p. 155), Lyon's *Urania* (1760), Bayley's *A New and Com-*

[3] George Hood, *A History of Music in New England* (Boston: Wilkins, Carter & Co., 1846), p. 9.

plete Introduction to the Grounds and Rules of Music (1764), and Billings' *The New England Psalm Singer: or American Chorister* (1770).

Among the "curious matter" included in this section is Hood's time-bound Victorian evaluation of Lyon's *Urania* in which he says:

> The arrangement of the harmony was bad, showing the editor to have been little acquainted with musical science. Dissonant chords are seldom used. In a few cases, the chord of the added sixth may be found at a cadence; and in a few more, the strange idea of a seventh taken at the cadence on the subdominant; but in no instance is one found on the dominant. This work contained the first music of a fuguing style ever published in this country. . . . The anthems were characterized by poor attempts at fugue and imitation with long runs in the melody.[4]

Hood's implicit charge that the harmonic and contrapuntal writing was excessively simple and conservative is best answered by Lyon as he addresses himself in his dedication, "To the Clergy of every Denomination in America" (p. 160). In this dedication Lyon refers to the goals to be reached by his publication, and these stated goals do provide some rationale for conservative settings.

Another "curious matter" is Hood's cautious evaluation of Billings' work both as a composer and as a theorist. He says of Billings' talent: "The tunes

[4] Hood, p. 160.

possessed considerable variety in character, and
more variety in metre, than any previous work. In
the harmony he took all the liberties one could
desire, either with or without knowledge."[5] Hood
also comments on Billings' essay "To all Musical
Practitioners." Hood writes, *"Nature is the best
Dictator,* [italics by Hood] for all the hard dry
studied Rules that ever were prescribed, will not
enable any person to form an Air. . . . It must be
Nature, Nature must lay the foundation, Nature
must inspire the Thought."[6] Hood's genteel view-
point of purity and nature have caused him to
select some of Billings' remarks which like his own
are timebound statements connected with contemporary continental music aesthetics.

The second part of the second section (1770–
1799) is a "list of works published before 1800."
They number 44 publications of tune and lesson
books, 18 of which are entitled *Harmonies.* The
first work is characteristically enough entitled *The
American Harmony,* and the last one is called
Harmonia Coelestis.

The third section, entitled "Origin of Choirs,"
is a condensed statement about the formation of
singing societies or schools which fostered the
organization of choirs. Hood has taken examples
from the church records of Rowley, Worcester, and
Ipswich, Massachusetts. In this section Hood also

[5] Hood, p. 168.
[6] Hood, p. 168.

treats the controversies which deal specifically with the lining-out practice.

The fourth section also has two parts. The first contains biographical sketches and is entitled "The Reformers" (pp. 202–218), and the second part is called "American Psalmists" (pp. 219–250). In the section on "American Psalmists" Hood sometimes combines a biographical sketch of the psalmist with some specimens of his poetry.

This fourth section of the book also makes some attempt to round off the work since it makes ample references to material discussed in the first section. The first paragraph of the first chapter of the first biography (p. 202), for example, shows the genteel quality of Hood at its most pronounced. Here he delights himself in viewing all things as if through the eyes of God. We are given a revelation of God's great plan for a new Zion, an eschatological glimpse of the unfolding fulfillment of the new "promised land." Not unlike a nineteenth-century Moses, Hood points the way when he portrays God as a provider of agents who perform His work through the church (p. 202) and through His music (p. 1). God has selected America where the church will "be more pure . . . " and will "be prepared for the latter-day glory . . . " having "raised up men . . . like [John] Cotton," Thomas Symmes, Solomon Stoddard, Peter Thacher, John and Samuel Danforth, and Nathaniel Chauncey.

The biographical sketches in Hood's book, then,

are not, when viewed from his vantage of a privileged destiny, tangents to the history of music he set out to present. On the contrary, in these biographical sketches Hood intends us to see proof of God's great plan. These little sketches also help to confirm Lowell Mason's evaluation of Hood's work: it is "well worthy the attention of all who feel an interest in the cause of church music, or who reverence the character of the Pilgrim Fathers." Or as Mason's long-time coeditor of nineteenth-century tune books, George J. Webb, expressed in his testimonial, "Its intrinsic value, however, consists in its being a medium to us of many excellent admonitions and teachings of great and good men of a former generation, on the uses and abuses of church music."

The fervor of Hood's admiration for his subjects burns through. Hood describes Sewall as, "humble, deliberate, cautious, and courageous; fearing nothing but sin."[7] "Cooper [is] the amiable, lovely friend; the practical evangelical, solemn and eminently successful preacher,"[8] and "Coleman [is] the amiable, and venerable man; the graceful and persuasive orator, the useful citizen, the friend of man, and the child of God."[9] These hero-like men are an intellectual force in the history of church music, the best friends of those who struggle and

[7] Hood, p. 217.
[8] Hood, p. 217.
[9] Hood, p. 217.

strive in the work of improving "the songs of Zion." From Hood's short descriptions of these twenty clergymen emanates a happiness, force, and energy which fills the reader with respect and nostalgia. Indeed, an almost transcendental quality is evident when Hood says of John Eliot:

> Amid the excitements and hurry of the present age we are too prone to neglect the memory of great and good men of other days and the lessons of wisdom illustrated in their lives. But a few scores of years, or even centuries, should not destroy our interest in their history, especially, when intimately connected with the youth of our country. Yet how seldom are those worthies mentioned, who in the infancy of the American colonies, laid the foundation of whatever is most valuable in our institutions! Few have been the points of time when the church and the world were blessed with so many worthy and excellent men.[10]

The stress on education, on moralizing didacticism, and the concern for instruction of the young is, of course, a result of the author's optimism, a positive quality of his genteel worldview. Every fact or date is presented in such a way that it can be "used," that it will add to our knowledge, that it will "advance" music and "encourage" the church. Each fact is so presented that it fulfills Hood's two objectives: (1) the collection and diffusion of musi-

[10] Hood, *A History of Music* . . .pp. 221–222.

cal knowledge, and (2) the cultivation and improvement of the style of church music. Because he is a pragmatic educationist, Hood uses repetition as a means of instruction and cites several versions of Psalm 1: Ainsworth (p. 14), Bay Psalm Book (p. 22), Dunster-Lyon (p. 27), Barnard (pp. 240–241), Prince (pp. 243–244); of Psalm 23: Ainsworth (p. 16), Bay Psalm Book (p. 23), Dunster-Lyon (p. 28), Prince (p. 244). Moreover, he likes to quote rules, to reproduce sermons in full, to dedicate a whole chapter to an evaluative annotated bibliography, and to give accounts of the sources used. It is characteristic that he extracts a paragraph from Cotton Mather's *The Accomplished Singer* which stresses the desirability of the education of the young:

> But in the pursuance of this holy intention, it would be very desirable, that people (and especially our young people who are most in the years of discipline,) would more generally learn to sing, and become able to *sing* by *rule,* and keep up the *notes* of the *tunes,* which our spiritual songs are set unto; which would be to sing agreeably and melodiously.[11]

Hood believed so firmly in music education for the young that he participated in a number of conferences on music instruction sponsored by the Boston Academy of Music and given by the two

[11] Hood, p. 110, quoting Cotton Mather, *The Accomplished Singer* (Boston: 1721).

famous professors of the Academy, Lowell Mason and George Webb. The first (1835) of these lectures was designed to illustrate the Pestalozzian method of teaching vocal music in classes, as contained in Mason's *Manual of the Boston Academy of Music, for Instruction in the Elements of Vocal Music*,[12] and to illustrate different styles of church music, taste, and methods of performance.[13]

The third convention, held in 1836, issued ten resolutions: (1) and (2) proposed to introduce music education into elementary education. The next seven resolutions were dedicated to the needs of sacred music education in general: (3) the cultivation of sacred music as an aid to devotion; (4) the need of trained choir directors; (5) the need for performance of non-difficult music; (6) the need for cooperation between teachers and choristers; (7) the need for untiring perseverance in the educational task; (8) that the position of a choir member is respectable, honorable, dignified and an ordinance established by God; (9) that a teacher of sacred music or a chorister must have a good, moral character. The tenth resolution was an expression of gratitude to Mason and Webb.[14]

It is characteristic that the early music conventions in this country showed a concern for both

[12] Robert T. John, "Origin of the first Music Educators' Convention, *Music Educator's Journal for Research in Music Education* (Winter, 1965), p. 208.

[13] *Ibid.*

[14] *Ibid.*, pp. 210–211.

public and church music education, though stress-
ing the latter. This collaboration of public and
church music education is symptomatic of the times.
It is not a peculiar prejudice of Hood alone, but
rather an unchallenged view held by leading contemporary figures. Even theories of learning were
not complete without the third "avenue of human
knowledge," faith. Mason has written:

> The teacher in pursuance of the right method, is
> guided by nature; he looks . . . to the intuitions,
> instincts, and opening faculties of active powers
> of his pupils . . . the pupil must know a thing
> through his perceptive power . . . the three grand
> avenues of human knowledge are the immediate
> *perception of the senses,* the *reasoning power,*
> and *faith.*[15]

It is also consistent with this belief that in the
Juvenile Lyre (by Lowell Mason and Elam Ives,
Jr.) music is described as appropriate "for the use
of Primary and Common Schools" if it consists of
"Hymns and Songs, Religious, Moral, and Cheerful." Moreover, the *Juvenile Lyre* lists the benefits
or effects which accrue from singing. These conse-
quential effects range from biological to intellectual
and spiritual. Significantly, it is the spiritual benefits which are first mentioned.

It is not surprising then that Hood dedicates the

[15] Lowell Mason, *A Brief Presentation of the Elementary Principles of Music* (New York: Ditson, 1871), p.
186.

entire first section of his book to the history of the regular singing movement, i.e., to the need of improving the reasonableness of singing, an improvement which he believes can be attained only through instruction. Hood is so contaminated by the spirit of reform in music education that he writes about the reform of music education in the generations preceding his. Reform and change are actually the main theme of his work. Discussions, debate, pleas, sermons make up the core of his work and show that he is more a teacher, a moral didactic among teachers, than a historian. Long sections of his book are devoted to the kinds of issues raised at the third class-convention, held in 1836. To explain the need for sacred music education, he includes long passages from Symmes' *The Reasonableness of Regular Singing, or Singing by Note* (1720); Hood feels the establishment of singing schools can fulfill the need for this kind of education.

Hood is especially concerned with the role of the clergy in music education. He admonishes his fellow clergymen to improve church music in the manner he believes clergymen once did:

> The clergy prepared, and preached upon the duty of improving their church music, with the same directness and pungency, as upon other subjects of Christian duty. . . . The church music of our forefathers before the Reformation in 1720, was held as most sacred. The tunes were supposed to

be holy; "and that as much reverence should be shown to them, as to the psalms themselves." It was the custom of the people, "to put off their hats, and put on a great show of devotion and gravity, whenever psalm tunes were sung, though there were not one word of a psalm."[16]

This statement is not in discord with the way Hood sees music flourishing in the land of peace:

Music dwells not in scenes of contention; she flies the abode of anarchy and confusion, and seeks a home in the land of peace. It is there, and there only, she dispenses her blessings.[17]

The privileged place of music in the Holy scheme of things is accented by Hood's inclusion of the essay, "Singing the Songs of the Lord" (pp. 123–137). In this essay, written in 1727, the Reverend Nathaniel Chauncey uses procedural language and attitudes of the worship service itself to argue in favor of regular singing. The Reverend Mr. Chauncey is directing his efforts to a solution of the controversy, as he states it: *"Whether in singing the Songs of the Lord, we ought to proceed by a certain Rule, or to do it in any loose, defective, irregular way, that this, or that people, have accustomed themselves unto?"*[18] Chauncey then proceeds

[16] Hood, pp. 143–144, and quoting Thomas Symmes, *The Reasonableness of Regular Singing, or Singing by Note* (Boston: 1720), p. 18.

[17] Hood, p. 84.

[18] Hood, p. 125, quoting Chauncey, "Singing the Songs of the Lord" (Durham, Conn.: 1727).

in his attempt to conquer those who oppose regular singing. His method is to state three premises or axioms to which, he concludes, "everyone will readily concede and grant,"[19] and from these deduce the logical and correct way, i.e., the will of God. Thus, Chauncey becomes a latter-day Moses leading his people to new heights in the promised land by the sure paths of reason. Regular singing is not only endorsed, its pronunciation has the ring of a creed. And this creed has the assurance and eloquence of having been wrung from a syllogism.

Obviously Hood identifies himself with this position. Nor can his position be taken lightly since Hood is one of the few ministers of his era who is knowledgeable in the areas of religion and music. Yet Hood's position is more implicit than explicit. He selects and promotes his champions and their causes. Hints that he is committed to this cause lie in a statement such as, "The next effort for the improvement of Psalmody in New England, was in 1718 when Dr. Cotton Mather published his 'Psalterium Americanum.' "[20] This statement immediately follows a section dealing with the Reverend John Tuft's book, *A Very Plain and Easy Introduction to the Art of Singing Psalm Tunes* (1721). It is then to be assumed that Tuft's book, which introduces the "new plan, in which *letters* are used

[19] Hood, p. 128, quoting Chauncey, *op. cit.* (footnote 18).

[20] Hood, pp. 67–68.

upon the staff instead of *notes*,"[21] i.e., the fa, so, la system, is the first effort in improving psalmody in New England. Hood also commits himself to regular singing when he endorses the reform efforts of "the best and ablest men of the Colonies"[22] in 1721 as "the first direct effort at improving their church music."[23]

It becomes increasingly clear that Hood regards music in the seventeenth century, like government, incipient capitalism, and the several art forms, as inseparable from church theology. His emphasis on the problems of the lining-out practice shows indirectly the great struggle which took place between the leaders and the led, the clergy and the congregation, the clerk and the choir. As the clergy intuited that the led were in fact leading by embellishing, trilling, quavering, twisting ad infinitum, a purifying movement, regular singing, arose to give the control back to the original leaders. Although by theme the opposite of the evangelical revivals to appear from 1734 through 1800, and acclaimed favorably by Hood, regular singing may be said to reflect similar ecclesiastical concern with a falling away of the church polity from interest in and adherence to the word of God.

Emerging throughout Hood's presentation is the

[21] Hood, p. 66, quoting John Tufts, *A Very Plain and Easy Introduction to the Art of Singing Psalm Tunes* (Boston: 1721).

[22] Hood, p. 85.

[23] Hood, p. 82.

image of a new people who face a bitter struggle for possession of their claimed property and right to freedom. These people are, inevitably, lively, spirited, enterprising, and dynamic, far excelling the "stay at home" types back in England. These characteristics are clearly reflected in the "ordered" reasonableness of regular singing. Even music in the homes was controlled and ordered. Eventually, however, the boyish *Weltanschauung* of the people balked at the controls and orders, making necessary the publication of many essays, rules, sermons, lectures, and addresses.

The music of eighteenth-century New England, we learn from Hood, reflects the religious diversification of the Eastern colonies. By the end of the century a great number of tune books for cities and villages, singing societies, private devotions, and worship services had been published. By the end of the century a great number of respectable and recognized composers and compilers were living in New England. The list includes such names as William Billings, Andrew Law, Asahel Benham, Jacob French, Abraham Wood, Daniel Read, Justin Morgan, Oliver Holden, Jacob Kimball, Supply Belcher, Samuel Babcock, Elias Mann, Timothy Swan, and Samuel Holyoke. They wrote anthems which were marked by the concept of a more immediate or imminent relationship between man and his God, and by a stress on strong sensation to awaken lucid perceptions. They favored a fugu-

HISTORY OF MUSIC IN NEW ENGLAND.

The history of music in New England, for the first two centuries, is the history of Psalmody alone; and this is so intimately connected with the history of the church, that he who would fully know the one, must understand the other. Between music and religion, in the churches of our land, there has ever been a beautiful and intimate connection. Like the wheels in Ezekiel's vision of the cherubim, "when they stood, these stood; and when they were lifted up, these lifted up themselves also." As religion waned amid the prosperity and specious errors of a growing country, so music was neglected; and as it revived, the voice of song was renewed. They have ever been reciprocating friends. Music has lent her aid, and religion has sanctified her services.

In order to know what the music of the Puritans was, we must go back to the history of music in

England at that time. Metrical Psalmody, it is well known, originated with the reformation ; and is the offspring of Luther's noble and devoted heart. He first used it in public service in the year 1517. Luther was a poet and a musician, — a man of great learning, refined taste, and possessing remarkable judgment and foresight. Knowing the power of music over the feelings, he used it to band together his followers, and inspire them with his own zeal. But the deep and ardent piety of his heart, could not venture upon the use of music indiscriminately. It must have enough of zest and enthusiasm in the melody to excite the feelings, while the words must be devotional to hallow the heart. But such music he found not ; and at once, from his energizing mind, he brought forth the choral, complete in all its magnificent beauty. A melody, free, symmetrical, and full of power, formed for the use of congregated thousands, and words fraught with the doctrines of the reformation, or full of deep and ardent devotion. Perhaps there is no better proof of his good taste, sound judgment, and deep piety, than the style of his music. Free in its melody compared with any then in use, it partook nothing of the vulgar and irreverent lightness of our so-called " revival music," a style as hostile to the progress of true religion, as it is to the cultivation of good taste.

Such was the character of the music of the reformation in Germany ; and to whatever country the reformation was carried, thither also was taken its favorite music.

In England, from the reformation onward to the close of Queen Elizabeth's reign, music was much cultivated. Every department had able composers. But choral music received particular attention. Some of the finest specimens of chorals are from the English masters. With little change, this style prevailed in the churches of England, and was brought by the puritans to this country.

It would be foreign to our design to speak of the effort to enlarge and improve the psalmody in the churches of England. It must suffice to say, that several manuals of Psalmody had been prepared before the puritans came to this country, the principal of which were those by Sternhold and Hopkins, and Henry Ainsworth.

THE PURITAN'S MANUAL OF PSALMODY.

When the puritans came to this country in 1620, their manual of Psalmody was a 1620. small, neat edition of Ainsworth's version of the Psalms. This was universally used in the New

England Colonies, until the New England version, or, as it was generally called, " The Bay Psalm Book," was completed by the clergy of the colonies in 1640.

In a library given by Rev. Thomas Prince, the Chronologist, to the Old South Church in Boston, (which may now be seen in the rooms of the Massachusetts Historical Society,) is a copy of Ainsworth, once used in the church at Plymouth. On the blank side of the title page is endorsed : " T. Prince. Plymouth, May 1, 1732 ; " and appended to it, in the chronologist's own hand-writing, is this note : " I have seen an edition of this version (published) in 1618 in quarto ; and this version of Ainsworth was sung in Plymouth Colony, and I suppose in the rest of N. E. 'till the New England version was printed in 1640." In a " Joco Serious Dialogue," upon music, written by the Rev. Thomas Symmes, of Bradford, Mass., " Concerning Regular Singing," printed at Boston in 1723, we find this additional information. " Furthermore (as is evident from a Psalm Book of Elder Chipman's now in my hands,) the Church at Plymouth, (which was the first Church in N. E.) made use of Ainsworth's version of the Psalms until the year 1692. For altho' our N. E. version of the Psalms was composed by sundry hands, and

completed by President Dunster, about the year
1640; yet that church did not use it, it seems, till
two and fifty years after, but stuck to Ainsworth;
and until about 1682, their excellent custom was
to sing *without* reading the line."

AINSWORTH'S VERSION.

Ainsworth's [1] version was entitled, " *The Book
of Psalmes: Englished both in Prose and Metre.
With annotations opening the words and sentences, by conference with other Scriptures. By
Henry Ainsworth. Eph.* 5. 18, 19. *Bee yee
filled with the Spirit; speaking to yourselves in
Psalms, and Hymns, and spiritual Songs: singing and making melodie in your hearts to the
Lord.*"

In " A Preface, declaring the reason and use of
this Booke," he says, " I have enterprised (Christian reader) this work, with regard of Gods honour,
and comfort of his people; that his word might
dwell in us richly, in all wisdom; and that we
might teach and admonish ourselves, in Psalmes
and hymnes and songs spirituall. This I have la-

---

[1] Rev. Henry Ainsworth was a puritan, and a writer and annotator
of celebrity, who flourished in England about the year 1600. See
biography.

boured to effect, by setting over into our tongue the Psalmes in metre, as agreeable to the originall Hebrew, as are other usuall translations. For the better discerning hereof, I turned them also into prose, and set these versions one by another, to be the more easily compared. And because the Psalms, have hard words, and phrases; I have added notes to explain them with brevity; which was to me as laborious, as if I had made a larger commentary."

This version was printed with the melodies in which they were to be sung, placed over the psalms. The music was printed in the lozenge or diamond shaped note, without bars, and was in the German choral style.

The following psalms are introduced as specimens of the poetry; and the first, to exhibit the manner in which they were all printed with the prose translation.

POETRY FROM AINSWORTH.

PSALM I.

1. O Blessed *is* the man, that doeth not walk, in the counsell of the wicked, nor stand in the way of sinners: nor sit in the seat of the scornfull.

PSALM I.

1. O Blessed man, that doth not in the wickeds counsell walk: nor stand in sinners way; nor sit in seat of scornful-*folk*.

2. But hath his delight, in the law of Iehovah, and in his law doeth meditate, day and night.

3. And he shall be as a tree, planted by brooks of waters : which shall give his fruit, in his time ; and his leaf shall not fade ; and whatsoever he-shall doe, shall prosper.

4. Not so, the wicked ; but as the chaff, which the wind driveth it-away.

5. Therefore the wicked shall not stand up, in the judgment : and sinners, in the assembly of the just.

6. For Jehovah knoweth, the way of the just : and the way, of the wicked shall-perish.

2. But *setteth* in Jehovahs law
    his pleasureful delight
    and in his law doth meditate,
    by day and eke by night.

3. And he shall be, like-as a tree,
    by water brooks planted ;
    which in his time, shall give his fruit
    his leaf eke [1] shall not fade ;
    and whatsoever he shall doe,
    it prosp'rously shall thrive.

4. Not so the wicked : but as chaff,
    which winde away-doth drive.

5. Therefore, the wicked shall not in
    the judgment stand-upright :
    and in th' assembly of the just,
    not any sinfull-wight.

6. For, of the just, Iehovah he
    acknowledgeth the way :
    and way of the ungracious
    shall utterly-decay.

PSALM VIII.

2. O Jah our Lord, how excellent-great *is*
    thy name in all the earth : thou which hast given
    thy glorious-majesty above the heaven.

3. From mouth of Babes, and sucklings, thou firmnes
    foundest ; because of them that thee distress :

    To make the foe, and self-avenger cease.

4. When I behold thy heav'ns thy fingers deed :
    the moon and starrs, which thou hast stablished.

5. What *is* frail-man that him thou remembrest ?
    and Adams Son, that him thou visitest ?

[1] Also.

6.   For thou a little lesser hast made him,
        than *be* the Gods : and crownd him with glory,
        and-eke *with* honorable-decency.
 7. Of thy hand-works, thou gavest him ruling :
        under his feet, thou set didst every-thing.

8.   Sheep and beeves all : and field-beasts with the same.
9. Fowl of the heav'ns, fish of the sea also :
        that through the path-waies of the seas doth go.
10. O Jah our Lord : how excellent-great-fame
        in all the earth, *hath* thy renowned-name.

PSALM XXIII.

1.   IEhovah feedeth me, I shall not lack.
2.   In grassy folds, he down doth make me lye :
        he gently-leads me, quiet waters by.
3. He doth return my soul : for his name sake,
        in paths of justice leads-me-quietly.

4.   Yea though I walk in dale of deadly-shade,
        ile fear none ill ; fore with me thou *wilt be :*
        thy rod thy staff eke, they shall comfort me.
5. Fore me, a table thou hast ready-made ;
        in their presence that my distressers be :

        Thou makest fat mine head with oynting-oil ;
        my cup abounds. 6. Doubtless, good and mercie
        shall all the dayes of my life follow me :
        also within Iehovahs house, I shall
        to length of dayes, repose-me-quietly.

PSALM LXX.

2. O, God for to deliver me :
    Iehovah, to mine helpe make-hast.
3. They that of my soule seekers be,
    ashamed be they and abasht.
    be backward turnd and blush doe they
    that in mine evill take delight.
4. Let them turne-backe, ha, ha, that say ;
    their bashfull-shame for to requite.

5. Ioy let them and rejoyce in thee,
    all that thee seeke : and let them say
    that thy salvations lovers bee,
    God magnified be, alway.
6. And I afflicted am and poore,
    O, God to me make speedy way :
    mine help and my deliverer
    thou *art ;* O Lord doe not delay.

PSALM C.

1. Showt to Jehovah, all the earth
2. Serve ye Jehovah with gladnes :
    before him come with singing-mirth
3. Know that Jehovah he God *is :*

    Its he *that* made us, and not wee ;
    his folk, and sheep of his feeding.
4. O with confession enter yee
    his gates, his courtyards with praising :

confesse to him, blesse ye his name.
Because Jehovah *he* good *is :*
  his mercy ever *is the same :*
  and his faith, unto all ages.

PSALM CXXXIV.

1. Behold, blesse ye the LORD,
     all ye the LORDS servants :
     that in the LORDS house stand, by nights.
3. O lift ye up your hands,

     within the holy-place :
     and blesse the LORD doe ye.
3. The LORD that made the heav'ns and earth ;
     blesse, out of Sion, thee.

PSALM CXXXVII.

1. By Babel's rivers there sate wee
     yea wept : when wee did mind, Sion.
2. The willowes *that* amidds it *bee :*
     our harps, we hanged *them* upon.
3. For songs of us, there ask did they
     that had us captive led-along ;
     and mirth, they that us heaps did lay :
     Sing unto us some Sions song.

4. Jehovahs song how sing shall wee ;
     within a forreyn-peoples land ?
5. Jerusalem, if I doe thee
     forget : forget let my right hand.

6. Cleave let my tongue to my palat,
   if I doe not in mind thee bear :
   if I Jerusalem doe not
   above my chiefest joy, prefer.

7. Remember LORD, to Ædom's sonns,
   day of Jerusalem : who sayd,
   rase, rase, to her-foundations,
8. Daughter of Babel, wastful layd :
   ô blessed he that thy reward
   payes thee, which thou rewardest us.
9. O blessed he, that takes, and hard
   against the Rock thy babes doth crush.

"THE BAY PSALM BOOK."

The puritan clergy of this country were esteemed in England, as eminent for scriptural knowledge, piety, and strict adherence to the word of God. As early as 1636, there had arrived in the colonies about thirty ministers, remarkable for their learning and piety. In 1640, these had composed and published a new version of ^{1640.} the Psalms.

In Mather's Magnalia, book iii. p. 100, may be found the following account of this work. "About the year 1639, the New English Reformers, considering that their churches enjoyed the other ordinances of Heaven in their spiritual purity, were

willing that the ordinance of singing psalms should
be restored among them unto a share in that purity.
Though they blessed God for the religious endeavours of them who translated the psalms into the
metre usually annexed, at the end of the Bible, yet
they beheld in the translation, variations of, not
only the text, but the very sense of the Psalmist,
that it was an offence unto them.   Resolving then
upon a new translation, the chief divines of the
country, took each of them a portion to be translated : among whom were Mr. Welds and Mr. Elliot of Roxbury, and Mr. Mather of Dorchester.
These like the rest were of so different a genius
for their poetry, that Mr. Shepard of Cambrige, on
the occasion addressed them to this purpose.

‘ You Roxbury Poets, keep clear of the crime
  Of missing to give us a very good rhyme.
  And you of Dorchester your verses lengthen,
  And with the texts own word you will them strengthen.’

" The psalms thus turned into metre, were printed
at Cambridge in the year 1640.   But afterwards it
was thought, that a little more art was to be employed upon them ; and for that cause they were
committed unto Mr. Dunster, who revised and
refined this translation ; and with some assistance
from one Mr. Richard Lyon, who being sent over

by Sir Henry Mildway, as an attendant unto his
son, then a student in Harvard College, and resid-
ing in Mr. Dunster's house, — he brought it into
the condition wherein our churches ever since have
used it."

The title of this version was, " *The Psalms in
Metre : Faithfully translated for the Use, Edification, and Comfort of the Saints in publick and
private, especially in New England.*" [1] — *Crown
8mo, of* 300 *pages.* It was printed in a clear,
new type, which was probably imported for that
particular work.[2] The preface is very lengthy ; and
the same was used for all subsequent editions, both
in this and in other countries. This first edition
contains only Psalms, there being no " Spiritual
songs," or hymns. At the close of the book was
the following

" ADMONITION TO THE READER."

" The verses of these psalmes may be reduced
to six kindes, the first whereof may be sung in very
neere fourty common tunes ; as they are collected
out of our chief musicians by *Tho. Ravenscroft.*

" The second kinde may be sung in three

---

[1] This version was known by two names — " The Bay Psalm
Book ; " and sometimes : " The New England Version."

[2] This was the first book printed in the Colonies.

tunes as *Ps.* 25, 50 and 67 in our english psalm books.

" The third, may be sung indifferently, as *ps.* the 51, 100 and ten commandments, in our english psalme books, which three tunes aforesaid, comprehend almost all this whole book of psalmes, as being tunes most familiar to us.

" The fourth as *ps.* 148, of which there but about five.

" The fift. as *ps.* 112 or the *Pater noster* of which there are but two, viz. 85, and 138.

" The sixt. as *ps.* 113, of which but one, viz. 115."

The following specimens will serve to illustrate the style of versification.

POETRY FROM THE BAY PSALMS.

PSALM 1.   BY ELLIOT, WELD AND MATHER.

1. O Blessed man, that in th' advice
      of wicked doeth not walk :
    nor stand in sinner's way, nor sit
      in charge of scornfull folk.
2. But in the law of Iehovah,
      is his longing delight :
    and in his law doth meditate
      by day and eke by night.

3. And he shall be like to a tree
    planted by water-rivers :
    that in his season yields his fruit,
      and his leafe never withers.
    And all he doth shall prosper well.
4.   The wicked are not so :
    but they are like vnto the chaffe,
      which winde drives to and fro.
5. Therefore shall not vngodly men,
    rise to stande in the doome,
    nor shall the sinner's with the just,
      in their assemblie *come*.
6. For of the righteous men, the Lord
    acknowledgth the way :
    but the way of vngodly men,
      shall vtterly decay.

PSALM 23. BY ELLIOT, WELD AND MATHER.

1. The Lord to mee a shepheard is,
    want therefore shall not I
2. He in the folds of tender grasse,
    doth cause me downe to lie :

    To waters calme mee gently leads
3.   Restore my soule doth hee :
    he doth in paths of righteousnes :
      for his names sake leade mee.

4. Yea though in valley of deaths shade
    I walk, none ill I'll feare :
    Because thou are with mee, thy rod,
      and staffe my comfort are.

5. Fore me a table thou hast spread,
    in presence of my foes :
  thou dost anoynt my head with oyle,
    my cup it over-flowes.

6. Goodnes and mercy surely shall
    all my dayes follow mee :
  and in the Lords house I shall dwelle
    so long as dayes shall bee.

PSALM 133. BY ELLIOT, WELD AND MATHER.

A Song of degrees, of David.

  1. How good and sweet to see,
      i'ts for bretheren to dwell
      together in unitee :
  2. It's like choice oyle *that fell*
      the head upon
      that downe did flow
      the beard unto
        beard of Aron :
      The skirts of his garment
      that unto them went down :
  3. Like Hermons dews descent,
      Sions mountaines upon,
        for there to bee
        the Lords blessing
        life aye lasting
        commandeth hee.

PSALM 134. BY ELLIOT, WELD AND MATHER.

1. O all yee servants of the Lord,
     behold the Lord bless yee :
   yee who within Iehovahs house
     i'th night time standing bee.
2. Lift up your hands, and blesse the Lord,
     in's *place* of holines.
3. The Lord that heav'n and earth hath made,
     thee out of Sion bless.

In 1647, a second edition was printed
with the same title and preface as the first. 1647.
To this a few "spiritual songs" were added, as
"The Song of Deborah," David's Elegy, &c.;
and many typographcial errors of the first edition
were corrected.

BAY PSLAM BOOK IMPROVED.

"After the second edition was published, the
rev. Henry Dunster, president of Harvard College,
and a master of Oriental languages, mr. Richard
Lyon, educated at a University in Europe, were
appointed a committee further to revise and improve the Psalms, which service they performed in
two or three years; when another edition was
published, with the addition of other scriptural

2

Songs." "Thomas's Hist. Printing," p. 233; also
" Mather's Magnalia."

1650.
In 1650, this revised edition was published
with the following title : *" The Psalms
Hymns and Spiritual Songs of the Old and
New Testament, faithfully translated into English Mertre, For the Use, Edification and Comfort of the Saints in publick and private, especially in New England. 2 Tim. 3, 16 and 17.
Col. 3, 16. Eph. 5, 18, 19. James 5, 13."*
8vo. 308 pages.

From this time it passed through edition after
edition, under many different forms, but without
any other alteration, till it was revised, in 1758,
by the Rev. Thomas Prince. It was reprinted in
England, in at least eighteen editions,[1] and was
preferred there, and in Scotland, by some eminent
congregations even as late as 1770. See the
Preface of Prince's edition.

In Scotland it passed through twenty-two editions, the twenty-second being printed in the year
1756. The writer has seen three editions published at Edinburg, by Alexander Kincaid, his

---

[1] "The Bay Psalm Book, 17th edition," was printed at London,
"by J. H. for T. Longman, at the Ship, in Pater Noster Row,
1737;" and the "18th edition, London, 1754," by the same publisher.

Majesty's printer : the eighteenth, in 1738, the twenty-first, in 1756, and twenty-second, in 1759. These had the preface of the American edition prefixed ; and were bound up with an edition of the Bible by the same printer.

As an example of the poetry of this improved edition, we give the 1st, 23d, and 137th Psalms. And here we would say, let not the reader wonder at the Vandal-like style of the poetry in this, and the previous examples. Sacred lyrics at that day, were, one might think, transposed to see how far they could be driven from their natural order. This work, however, is a great improvement upon that of Ainsworth, yet, he was a scholar, a writer, a critic, and produced a work, as a whole, vastly superior to those of his predecessors, Seager, Sternhold and Hopkins, and others.

SPECIMENS OF THE BAY PSALM BOOK IMPROVED.

PSALM 1.   IMPROVED BY DUNSTER AND LYON.

1. O blessed man that walks not in
    th' advice of wicked men
   Nor standeth in the sinner's way
    nor scorners seat sits in.
2. But he upon Jehovah's law
    doth set his whole delight :
   And in his law doth meditate
    Both in the day and night.

3. He shall be like a planted tree
    by water brooks, which shall
  In his due season yield his fruit,
    whose leaf shall never fall :
  And all he doth shall prosper well.
  4. The wicked are not so :
  But they are like unto the chaff,
    which wind drived to and fro.
5. Therefore shall not ungodly men
    in judgement stand upright.
  Nor in th' assembly of the just
    shall stand the sinfull wight.
6. For of ye righteous men ye LORD
    acknowledgeth the way :
  Whereas the way of wicked men
    shall utterly decay.

PSALM 23.   IMPROVED BY DUNSTER AND LYON.

  The Lord to me a sheperd is,
    want therefore shall not I.
  He in the folds of tender grass,
    doth make me down to lie.
  He leads me to the waters still,
    Restore my soul doth he ;
  In paths of righteousness, he will
    for his name's sake lead me.

  In valley of death's shade although
    I walk, I'll fear none ill :
  For thou with me thy rod, also,
    thy staff me comfort will.

Thou hast 'fore me a table spread,
  in presence of my foes :
Thou dost anoint with oil my head,
  my cup it over-flows.

Goodness and mercy my days all
  shall surely follow me :
And in the LORD's house dwell I shall
  so long as days shall be.

PSALM 137. IMPROVED BY DUNSTER AND LYON.

By water floods of Babylon
  there have we sitten down :
Yea there we mourned, when as we
  did Sion think upon.
Our harps in midst of her we did
  hang willow trees among,
For there they us who captive led
  required of us a song :

Who laid us waste, askt mirth, sing us
  a Sion's song do ye.
How in a land of strangers sing
  Jehovah's song shall we?
O, thou Jerusalem, if I
  of thee forgetful be :
Then let my right hand quite forget
  her own dexterity.

If I thee mind not, let my tongue
  not from my palat move :
If I set not Jerusalem
  my chiefest joy above.

The design of the versifiers of the Bay Psalm Book, was to produce a metrical translation, nearer to the original than those then in use. In this they succeeded. Theirs was a *literal* translation. Many similar attempts had been made before, but no one had proved so successful. Their numbers were generally worse, while they had more violations of the text; and this, to our Puritan fathers, was the fault of faults. This work, as a faithful translation, was highly esteemed, both in England and Scotland, and was reprinted in each in large and frequent editions. In Scotland it was published by his Majesty's printer; and large numbers were bound up with the Bible, and sold in this country. The writer has seen many copies from one hundred to one hundred and fifty years old. Editions of the Scotch reprint are common.

Its faults, as a metrical version, designed to be sung, were many and palpable. But, at that day, it had no rival; and is it venturing too much to say, that under the same restrictions, it could have few, if any, now? — Theirs was indeed a difficult task — *a close literal translation, in measure and in rhyme!* We venture the assertion, that *no one, with those requirements has equalled it.*[1]

---

1 This translation has been considered by a Hebraist, as equal, if not superior to, the version in the Bible.

Those who made more pleasing numbers, fell far short of their conformity to the text ; while those who made the smoothest and most desirable numbers, have merely paraphrased, imitated, or drawn their subjects from the Bible. Watts is but a paraphrase. Addison's beautiful samples in the lines beginning, "The spacious firmament on high," and "The Lord my pasture shall prepare," of what he intended, and of what he could have prepared so ably, namely, a complete metrical version of the Psalms, were but a free translation or paraphrase.

In this work there was little variety of measure, though more than in any previous version. The principal metres were the Short, Common, Long, and Tens. The 10s are regular iambics, of which, a few specimens have stanzas of five lines each. Some of the psalms were of immoderate length, containing sixty, seventy, a hundred, and even one hundred and thirty lines. These were sung at one standing,[1] though sometimes occupying a full half hour. The hundred and fifty psalms divided as they were, made about two hundred and fifty parts ; and of these only *twenty-five*, or one in ten, was any other than Common, or *the metre*. Of

[1] In those days, they performed their highest devotional act *standing*.

these twenty-five, some half dozen were written in
the Hallelujah metre, or four lines of six, and four
of four syllables. The remaining eighteen or
twenty were mostly in Long metre.

The lines had great license in regard to quantity,
some containing more, and some less, than they
should. This defect, they easily remedied in singing, by contracting or lengthening a word, as in
the following examples.

> " I' th' city of the Lord of Hosts."
> " This is the Lord on whom we had
>   Our expectation ;
>   We will rejoice, and will be glad
>   In his salvation."
>
> *Hymn of Isaiah, Chap.* 25.

See also the Song of Moses, which, as also the
above, would be measured.

> " Iah is my strength and song, and he
>   Is my sal-va-ti-on ;
>   He is my God and I'll prepare
>   an hab-i-ta-ti-on."

The few hymns that they had, as a supplement
to the Psalms, were no doubt, to them more
pleasing and devotional than we can well imagine.
But at this day, with our improved lyrics, we could
hardly deem it possible that such specimens as the

following, could ever have been used for devotional purposes.

> " Jael the Kenite, Heber's wife
>   'bove women blest shall be
> Above the women in the tent
>   a blessed one is she.
> He water ask'd, she gave him milk :
>   in lordly dish she fetch'd
> Him butter forth : unto the nail
>   she forth her left hand stretch'd :
>
> Her right hand to the workman's maul
>   and Sisera hammered :
> She pierc'd and struck his temples through,
>   and then cut off his head.
> He at her feet bow'd, fell, lay down,
>   he at her feet bow'd where
> He fell : whereas he bowed down
>   he fell distroyed there."
>
> *A part of the " Song of Deborah and Barak."*

This version, though made by the sanction of the church, was opposed by not a few. Among the early settlers of the colonies, there was much difference of opinion concerning the matter of singing.[1] Some believed, that Christians should not

---

[1] We copy the following extract from the "Encyclopedia of Religious Knowledge," just to show that the same difficulties existed in England ; and it was probably these that made the Westminster Assembly, not only insist upon the duty, but even provide for the

sing at all, but only praise God with the heart.
Others believed it right to sing, but thought it
wrong to sing the Psalms of David. Some believed

wants of their churches by giving them a new version of the Psalms,
which was prepared by one of their number, Mr. Rouse, whose name
the version still bears : —

"A curious controversy on this subject arose among the Dissenters
in the end of the seventeenth century. Whether singing in public
worship had been partially discontinued during the times of persecution to avoid informers, or whether the miserable manner in which
it was performed gave persons a distaste to it, so it appears, that in
1691, Mr. Benjamin Keach published a tract, entitled, " The Breach
Repaired in God's Worship : " or, Psalms, Hymns, &c. proved to be
a Holy Ordinance of Jesus Christ." To us it may appear strange
that such a point should be disputed ; but Mr. Keach was obliged to
labor earnestly, and with a great deal of prudence and caution, to
obtain the consent of his people to sing a hymn at the conclusion of
the Lord's Supper. After six years more, they agreed to sing on the
Thanksgiving days ; but it required still fourteen years more before
he could persuade them to sing every Lord's day ; and then it was
only after the last prayer, that those who chose it might withdraw
without joining in it ; nor did even this satisfy these scrupulous con-
sciences ; for, after all, a separation took place, and the inharmonious
seceders formed a new church in Maze Pond, where it was above
twenty years longer before singing the praises of God could be en-
dured. It is difficult at this period to believe it ; but Mr. Ivimey
quotes Mr. Crosby, as saying, that Mr. Keach's was the first church
in which psalm singing was introduced. This remark, however, must
probably be confined to the Baptist churches.

The Presbyterians, it seems, were not quite so unmusical ; for the
Directory of the Westminster divines distinctly stated, that " it is
the duty of Christians to praise God publicly by singing of psalms
together in the congregation." And besides the old Scotch psalms,
Dr. John Patrick of the Charterhouse, made a version, which was in
very general use among Dissenters, Presbyterians, and Independents,

it wrong for any but Christians to sing: and others thought one only should sing, while the assembly should join in silence, and respond Amen.

REV. JOHN COTTON'S TRACT.

To meet these differences of opinion the Rev. John Cotton in 1647 published a treatise on singing, entitled,

1647.

"*Singing of Psalms a Gospel ordinance : Or a treatise wherein are handled these four particulars. I. Touching the duty itself. II. Touching the matter to be sung. III. Touching the singers. IIII. Touching the manner of singing. By John Cotton, Teacher of the Church at Boston in New England.*"

The design of this work was to meet the objections to the use of a metrical translation of the Psalms; and to prepare the way for the Bay Psalm Book, then about to be published, as revised by President Dunster. It considered the duty, the

---

before it was superseded by the far superior compositions of Dr. Watts. These psalms, however, like those of the English and Scotch establishment, were drawled out in notes of equal length without accent or variety. Even the introduction of the triple-time tunes, probably about the time of Dr. Watts's psalms, gave also great offence to some people, because it marked the accent of the measure. Old Mr. Thomas Bradbury used to call this time "a long leg and a short one."

matter, the singers, and the manner of singing. His first point was to prove the duty of audible singing. The reason for this was, that at that time, there were those who believed that the scriptures, intended nothing more by the word *singing*, than thankfulness and joy of heart. Hence he says: " For the first Question, wee lay downe this conclusion for a Doctrine of Truth : *That singing* of Psalms with a lively *voyce, is an holy Duty of God's Worship now in the dayes of the New Testament.* When we say, singing with lively voyce, we suppose none will so farre misconstrue us, as to thinke wee exclude singing with the heart ; For God is a Spirit: and to worship him with the voyce without the spirit, were but lip-labor: which (being rested in) is but lost labour (Isa. 29. 13,) or at most, profiteth but little, 1 Tim. 4. 8. But this wee say, As wee are to make melody in our hearts, so in our voyces also. In opposition to this, there be some Antipsalmists, who doe not acknowledge any singing at all with the voyce in the New Testament, but onely [1] spirituall songs of joy and comfort of the heart in the word of Christ." His proofs were : —

1. " The commandments of the Lord by Paul."

[1] It was customary in those days to spell this word with the *e*; now we leave it out, forming the contraction "*only.*"

2. " The examples of Christ himself, and of his Saints and Deciples in the New Testament."

3. " The Prophecies of the Old Testament, foretelling and perswading such a dutie in the New.

" The second Question about singing of Psalms, *concerneth the matter of the Psalmes to be sung ;* for there be some who do not scruple singing with the voyce (as the former sort did) but singing of the Psalmes of *David* now in these dayes of the New Testament. As conceiving Davids Psalmes were penned for Temple worship, during the Pedagogy of the Old Testament. But now in the dayes of the *New Testament* when God hath promised to powre out his Spirit upon all flesh, now the whole worship of God should be carried on, not by set formes of Psalmes (no more than by set formes of prayer) but by personall spirituall gifts, whereby some one or other of the members of the church, having received a Psalme by the enditement of the Spirit, he singeth it openly in the publique Assembley of the Church, and the rest of the bretheren say Amen to it in the close."

" But touching the persons of those who should sing, it pertaineth to the third Question. This second Question chiefly concerneth the matter to be sung, whether the *Psalmes* of *David*, or some Psalme or Hymne, endited by personall gift of this

or that member of the Church.   Wherein we hold
and believe ;

1. " That not onely the Psalmes of David, but
any other spirituall songs recorded in Scripture,
may lawfully be sung in Christian Churches, as the
song of *Moses* and *Asaph, Heman* and *Ethan,
Solomon* and *Hesekiah, Habacuck* and *Zachary,
Hannah* and *Deborah, Mary* and *Elisebeth,* and
the like."

2. " Wee grant also, that any private Christian,
who hath a gift to frame a Spirituall Song, may both
frame it, and sing it privately, for his own private
comfort, and remembrance of some speciall benefit
or deliverance.   Nor doe we forbid the private use
of any Instrument of Musick therewithall ; So that
attention to the instrument, doe not divert the heart
from attention to the matter of the Song."

" Neither doe wee deny, but that in the publique
thanksgiving of the Church, if the Lord should furnish any of the members of the Church with a
spiritual gift to compose a *Psalme* upon any speciall occasion, he may lawfully be allowed to sing
it before the Church, and the rest hearing it, and
approving it, may goe along with him in the Spirit,
and say Amen to it."

" The reasons for our Faith and Practice are
these : 1. Taken from the Commandment or exhor-

tation of the Apostle, Ephes. 5. 19 : *Be you filled
with the Spirit* (saith he) *speaking to yourselves*
(that is, one to another) *in Psalmes and Hymnes
and Spirituall Songs, singing and making melody in your hearts to the Lord.* To the like purpose is his commandment and exhortation to the
Colossians, chap. 3, ver. 16. *Let the word of
Christ dwell in you richly in all wisdom, teaching
and admonishing one another, in Psalmes and
Hymnes and Spirituall Songs, singing with
grace in your hearts to the Lord.* In both which
places, as the Apostle exhorteth us to singing, so
he instructeth us what the matter of our Song
should be, to wit, *Psalmnes, Hymes* and Spirituall
Songs ; Now those three be the very Titles of the
Songs of *David,* as they are delivered to us by the
Holy Ghost himselfe ; some of them are called
Psalmes, some *Hymnes,* some Spirituall Songs.
Now what reason can be given why the Apostle
should direct us in our singing to the very titles of
Davids Psalmes, if it were not his meaning that
we should sing them ? Yea, either wee must exclude the *Psalmes* of *David* from the name of
Psalmes, and *Hymnes,* and Spirituall Songs ; or
else we must be forced to acknowledge, that we
are exhorted to sing them, as well as any other."

Here follow a long list of objections to the use

of the Psalms in Christian worship; with also their
appropriate answers.

The second argument in favor of using the
Psalms of David, was taken from *their end, and
use.* He says : —

" The Psalms of *David* and *Asaph*, and the like,
were written for a threefold end, as we see expressed by the Apostle, Col. 3. 16, to wit : 1. For
Instruction, or Teaching.   2. For Admonition.
3. For Singing Praise and Thanksgiving to the
Lord.

" Now if the *Psalms* of *David*, and the like,
were written (as doubtlesse they were) in the Old
Testament for this threefold end, and each of them
for morall (that is, for generall, and perpetuall use)
and none of them abrogated in the *New Testament*, look then, as it would be a sacrilegious sinne,
to take away from the *Psalms* either of the two
former uses (the use of Instruction, or Admonition ;) so it will be alike sacriledge to deprive them
of the threefold use, by forbidding them to be sung
for praise and thankesgiving to the Lord.   Whereto
a *third* Argument may be added, *taken from the
dutie of singing Psalmes every Sabbath*, and the
defect of provision of other *Psalmes*, if the Psalmes
of *David*, and other Scripture Psalmes be refused."

" The third Question about Singing of *Psalmes*,

concerneth the Singers. For though vocall singing be approved, and also the singing of *Davids
Psalms*, yet still it remaineth to some a question,
who must sing them. And here a threefold scruple
arriseth, 1. Whether one be to sing for all the rest,
the rest joyning onely in spirit, and saying Amen ;
or the whole Congregation ? 2. Whether women,
as well as men ; or men alone ? 3. Whether carnall men and Pagans may be permitted to sing with
us, or Christians alone, and Church-Members."

As it regards the *first* scruple, he argued that
all should sing; with liberty for *one* to sing a psalm
written by himself, while the church should respond
Amen.

"The second scruple about Singers is, *Whether
women may sing as well as men.* For in this
poynt, there be some that deale with us, as *Pharaoh*
dealt with the *Israelites*, who though he was at first
utterly unwilling that any of them should goe to
sacrifice to the Lord in the Wilderness, yet being
at length convinced that they must goe, then he
was content the men should goe, but not the women.
Ex. 10. 11. So here, some that were altogether
against singing of *Psalmes* at all with lively voyce,
yet being convinced, that it is a morall worship of
God warrented in Scripture, then if there must be

3

a Singing, one alone must sing, not all, (or if all)
the men onely, and not the women.

" And their reason is. 1. Because it is not permitted to a woman to speake in the Church,
1 Cor. 14, 34, how then shall they Sing? 2.
Much lesse is it permitted to them to prophecy in
the Church 1 Tim. 2, 11 & 12. And singing of
Psalmes is a kinde of Prophecying."

" The third scruple about the Singers remaineth, Whether carnall men and Pagans may be permitted to sing with us, or Christians alone, and
Church-members?

" What we believe on this poynt, may be sum-
med up in these three particulars.

1. " That the Church and the members thereof
are called to sing to the Praises of God and to their
mutuall edification: For they were Churches of
Christ, and members of Churches whom the Apostle exhorteth to speake to themselves, and make
melody to the Lord with Psalms and Hymns and
spirituall songs. Eph. 5. 19. Colos. 3. 16.

2. " That the praising of God with *Psalmes* is
comely for all the upright, whether received into the
Fellowship of any particular visible Church, or no.
For so much the words of *David* hold forth,
Praise is comely for the upright.

3. " Though spirituall gifts are necessary to

make melody to the Lord in singing; yet spirituall gifts are neither the onely, nor chiefe ground of singing; but the chiefe ground thereof is the morall duty lying upon all men by the commandement of God : *If any be merry to sing Psalmes.* Jas. 5, 13. As in Prayer, though spirituall gifts be requisite to make it acceptable; yet the dutie of prayer lyeth upon all men by that Commandement which forbideth Atheisme; it is *the foole that saith in his heart There is no God;* of whom it is said, *they call not upon the Lord*, Ps. 14, 1 – 4. Which also may serve for a just Argument and proofe of the point."

1. "If by the Commandment of God, and indeed by the light of Nature, all men be bound to pray unto God in their distresses, (as even Jonahs Marriners will confesse in a storme, Jonah 1, 6.) then all men are likewise bound to sing to the praise of God in their deliverences, and comforts; For the word runneth alike levell, *Is any afflicted, let him pray ? Is any merry ?* let him sing Psalmes. Jas. 5, 13."

His other arguments were drawn from the general commands to sing, from the sovereignty of God, and from the greatness and goodness of his works in creation and providence.

On the other hand, the objections were : that

scripture songs were sung only by the people of God — that singing is a public dispensation of the Word, and none but the truly pious have a right to dispense it — "that if pagans and profane persons may sing they may prophesy also in Christ's spiritual temple" — that a mixed assembly could only make confusion — that when the unregenerate sing, they must sing that not suitable to their own condition, &c. these being their principal arguments.

"The fourth and last head of Scruples remaineth, touching *the manner of singing.*

"1. *Whether it be lawfull to sing Psalmes in Meeter devised by men?*

"2. *Whether in Tunes invented?*

"3. Whether it be lawfull in Order unto Singing, to reade the Psalme?

"The two former of these Scruples, because they stand upon one and the same ground, may fitly be handled together.

"The judgment of the Churches of Christ in these Points, is doubtlesse suitable to their Practice, *That it is lawfull to sing Psalmes in English Verses* (which run in *number, measure* and meeter) *and in such grave and melodious tunes, as doe well befit both the holinesse and gravitie of the matter, and the capacitie of the Singers.*"

This proposition he argued on the ground ; that if it be right to translate the Hebrew Bible into English prose, in order to read, then it is equally proper to translate the Hebrew psalms into English verse to sing. And for the tunes to which they objected, he argued, that as it is right to use *words* invented by Englishmen to convey divine truth, so it is right to use *tunes* by them invented, for the same purpose.

The principal objection against the Psalms in verse was this : " The Meeter of the late Translators, though it come nearer to the Originall, then the former Meeters, yet not so neare as the Prose. They frame their words and sentences more to the Meeter then the Prose. Yea they sometimes breake the Attributes of God, and for the verse sake put *Jah* for *Jehovah :* which is a mangling of the word."

The objections against the tunes were ; that they were uninspired — that to sing man's melody is only a vain show of art — and that God could not take delight in praises when sinful man, or " the man of sin," " had a hand in making the melody."

To the last objection he gives this answer. " God delighteth that his will should be obeyed : at least he abhorreth that his will should be disobeyed,

though by sinfull men 1. Sam. 15. 22, 23.   Since
God commandeth all men in distresse to call upon
him, and all men in their mirth, to sing his Praise,
what is mortall sinfull man, (Dust and Ashes) that
he should forbid, what God hath commanded?
God knoweth how to allow, yea and to reward
what is his own : when yet he taketh no pleasure
in the sinfull manner of performance of any Dutie.
God tooke notice of *Ahabs* humiliation, and rewarded it with respite of temporall judgments,
though he tooke no pleasure in his sinfull hypoc-
risie.   And yet they that had a hand in making
Melody of the English *Psalmes* (whether in old
England or *New*) were men of a better spirit
than *Ahab*.   But I can but marveile, why you
should put in the man of sinne, as having any
hand at all, in making this Melody.   For neither
the man of sinne (by whom I suppose you meane
Antichrist) nor any Antichristian Church have had
any hand in turning *Davids Psalmes* into English
Songs and Tunes, or are wont to make any Melody
in Singing them, yea they reject them as *Genevah
Gigs ;*   And they be Cathedrall Priests of an Antichristian spirit, that have scoffed at Puritan-Minis-
ters, as calling the people to sing one of *Hopkins
Jiggs*, and so hop into the Pulpit.   God keep all
Anti-Psalmists from the like Antichristian Spirit.

They that have been in Antichristian Churches can tell you, that Popish Churches are not wont to sing *Davids Psalmes* translated into verse in their own Country Meeter, but they onely sing the Prose of *Davids Psalmes* in Cathedrall Notes. Which how farre yourself close withall, I leave to yourself to consider."

" The last scruple remaining in the manner of singing, Concerneth the order of Singing after the Reading of the Psalme. For it is doubted by some, and concluded by others, that reading the *Psalmes* is not to be allowed in order to singing. We for our parts easily grant, that where all have books and can reade, or else can say the *Psalme* by heart, it were needlesse then to reade each line of the Psalme beforehand in order to singing. But if it be granted, which is already proved, that the *Psalmes* to be ordinarily sung in Publique, are Scripture-*Psalmes*, and those to be sung by the body of the Congregation ; then to this end it will be a necessary helpe, that the words of the *Psalme*, be openly read beforehand, line after line, or two lines together, that so they who want either books or skill to reade, may know what is to be sung, and joyne with the rest in the dutie of sing-ing. It is no unwarrentable invention of man, brought into the worship of God, to make use of such meanes, which the light of Nature teacheth us, to be either necessary or convenient helpes, either to the hearing or understanding of what is said in the worship of God."

This recommendation of reading the psalms — "lineing out" — was objected against by many, as having no authority in the Scriptures — that the Bible prescribed no officer for reading — and that the "reading of the *Psalme* doth hinder the melody, the understanding, the affection in singing."

THE PURITAN'S PSALMODY.

The following remarks upon the Psalmody of this country are taken from "Thomas's History of Printing:" see vol. 1, p. 466. They are copied because he is generally so very correct in his statements; and because he has published an error, calculated to lead his readers to believe that other versions were used by our Puritan Fathers, beside those mentioned in the preceding pages. He says:

"It had been customary to sing a prose translation of the Psalms;[1] and for this purpose the

---

[1] There is almost a certainty that no other version than Ainsworth's was ever used in the colonies until the New England version was published. But if any one was used in one or two of the churches, it was Sternhold and Hopkins. The writer, after extensive research

psalms were marked for singing in lines to suit the tunes. To accommodate common metre tunes, two syllables in every other line were printed in black letter,[1] which were to be omitted when tunes of this metre were sung. The minister or deacon who read the psalm line by line as it was sung usually announced that the syllables in black, were or were not, to be omitted." Thus : —

> "So spake th' Eternal to my Lord ;
> Sit Thou (**enthron'd**) at my right hand,
> Until I make thine enemies
> A (**conquer'd**) footstool for thy feet."
>
> *Ps.* 110.

has never so much as seen the most distant allusion to one, except in "Felt's history of Ipswich," which says that Sternhold and Hopkins was used in the first church in that town. Ainsworth's was far enough from good rhythm, to make it prose, if that could do it ; but his was written in rhyme. Dr. Cotton Mather published a version in blank verse ; but he could not mean that, for he mentions it by name.

[1] Mr. Thomas is here again wrong. As it regards Common metre, it was *all* common — all the psalms being written in lines of eight syllables and six, alternately. They were so written in Ainsworth's and in the New England Psalm Book ; and their tunes were written so of course.

And as it regards the "black letter," the only version in which that was used, was Dr. Cotton Mather's *Psalterium Americanum*, or version in blank verse mentioned above ; and but few churches used this. In this a few psalms, nine, including the 119th, were thus prepared with the Black letter to be sung in Long Metre ; while the rest, like all other books, was written in Common Metre.

For more than a century " The Bay Psalm Book " was almost the only work used in the New England churches. During that time it passed through, nearly if not quite thirty editions. The twenty-sixth edition was printed at Boston in the year 1744.

The twenty-seventh edition may be seen in the Antiquarian Hall at Worcester, Mass. There is no date of the year in which it was published ; but it was probably done between the years 1746 and 1750. This work, including those published in Europe, must have passed through at least *seventy* editions.

MUSIC A COLLEGE STUDY.

The Psalmody of the church, received early and special attention, from our Puritan fathers. The Rev. Mr. Symmes in a discourse on " The Reasonableness of Regular Singing ; or Singing by Note," says : " It was studied, known and approved of in our College, for many years after its first founding. This is evident from the Musical Theses, which were formerly printed ; and from some writings containing some tunes, with directions for *singing by note*, as they are now sung : and these are yet in being [1] though of more than sixty years' standing." From this it would seem, that in the early history of the college, it was a regular study. The same author in speaking of the first settlers of New England, and their children, says, "There are many persons of credit now living, children and grandchildren of the first settlers of N. E. who can very well remember, that their ancestors sung by *note*, and they learned so to sing of them; and they have more than their bare words to prove that they speak the truth; for many of them can sing tunes exactly by note, which they learned of their Fore-fathers, and they say that they sung all the tunes after the same manner; and these people now sing those

---

[1] These, with the Theses and many valuable papers and books, were burnt with the college library. Had they remained until this day, materials for a history of our music would not have been so scarce, nor the history itself so meagre. We can, however, submit to such accidents; but when a ruthless hand coolly destroys all that connects us with the past, its history, in whatever form, it is thoughtlessness and ignorance intolerable. A Philosopher's dog, being left by accident in his master's study, overturned the lamp, set on fire the manuscripts, and destroyed in a moment, the accumulated labor of years. The Philosopher seeing the irreparable mischief, only exclaimed: "O, Diamond! Diamond! thou knowest not what thou hast done!" This to a brute was a proper exclamation. But when we see the devastation that is almost universally made, with old books, papers, and records, valuable for their historic information, by brutes in human form, what language is harsh enough to denounce such impious destruction?

tunes most agreeable to note, which have been least practiced in the congregation."

The music used for a long time before the year 1690, was mostly written in their Psalm Books, and had been so from the first using of the Bay Psalm Book. The number of tunes thus written rarely exceeded five or six. The music was principally taken from Ravenscroft's Collection [1] with little or no alteration; and this was used nearly one hundred years.

From the publication of the New England Psalms and Hymns in 1640, for fifty or sixty years, we have been able to find no positive information, that anything was done for the advancement of music. The Psalms and Hymns passed through edition after edition, as the wants of a growing country

[1] This collection had been published in England in 1618, two years before the Pilgrims came to this country. The harmonies being made by some of the best musicians in England, it soon became the standard work for the churches both in that country and in the colonies. These musicians were Thomas Tallis, Dr. John Dowland, Thomas Morley, Bachelor of Music, Gyles Farnaby, B. M., Thomas Tompkins, B. M., John Tompkins, B. M., Martin Pierson, B. M., William Parsons, Edmund Hooper, George Kirby, Edward Blanks, Richard Allison, John Farmer, Michael Cavendish, John Bennet, Robert Palmer, John Milton, Simon Stubbs, Richard Crawford, William Harrison, Thomas Ravenscroft, B. M. This work ascribes the composition of the parts of Old Hundred, to Dr. John Dowland. The melody is probably German.

demanded; but no alteration in the style of the version or provision for music was made.

The " Bay Psalm Book " was not used in the church at Salem until 1667. Some diffi- 1667. culties having occurred in that church, Ainsworth was continued up to the above date. The church then agreed to use the Bay Psalm Book, in connection with Ainsworth, as will be seen by the following extract from the records of the First Church of that city. " At a Church Meeting 4th of 5th month 1667 " or May 4th, " The pastor having formerly propounded and given reason for the use of *The Bay Psalm Book* in regard to the difficulty of the tunes, and that we could not sing them so well as formerly, and that there was a singularity in our using Ainsworth's tunes ; but especially because we had not the liberty of singing all the Scripture Psalm's according to Col. 3. 16. He did now again propound the same, and after several bretheren had spoken there was at last, a unanimous consent with respect to the last reason mentioned, that the Bay Psalm Book should be used together with Ainsworths to supply the defects of it."

The Bay Psalm Book was adopted by the First Church in Ipswich about the same time 1667. as by the church in Salem ; and was used nearly one hundred years.

In the year 1692, the church at Plymouth
1692.   adopted the "Bay Psalm Book;" and this
gave rise in that church, if not in others, to the
custom of reading the line, as was eighteen years
before recommended by the Westminster Assembly.

The following extract is copied from the Church
Records at Plymouth.   In 1685, " May 17,
1685.   the Elder stayed the church after the public
worship was ended, and moved to sing psalm 130th
in another translation, because in Mr. Ainsworth's
translation, which we sang, the tune was so difficult
few could follow it — the church readily concented
thereunto.

" June 19, 1692. The Pastor stayed the church
after meeting and propounded that seeing many of
the psalms in Mr. Ainsworth's translation, that we
now sung, had such difficult tunes, that none in
the church could set, that the church would consider of some way of accommodation, that we
might sing all the psalms, and left it to their consideration.

" Aug. 7th. At the conclusion of the Sacrament
the Pastor called upon the church to express their
judgments about this motion ; the vote was
1692.   this : when the tunes are difficult in the translation we use, we will sing the psalms now used in
our neighbor churches in the Bay ; — not one

brother opposed this conclusion. The Sabbath following, Aug. 14, we began to sing the psalms in course according to the vote of the church."

INDIAN PSALMS.

In 1661, Mr. Elliott had translated the Psalms into Indian verse, which was that ^{1661.} year printed with the New Testament by Mr. Green of Cambridge ; and when he had finished the Old Testament, they were all bound up together. It was entitled : " *Wame Ketoohomae Uketoohoma-ongash David.*" 4to.

The following specimen of this work is :

PSALM CXVII.

Waeenomok Maniz wame
wutohtimoneunk
Waeenomokkenaau wame
miffinninnuog wonk
2. Ummonaneteaonk miffi
en kuhhogkanonut
Wunnomwaonk God michemohtem
watenomook Maniz.

Several copies of this work can be seen in the Massachusetts Historical Library. It is also in many of the great Libraries in England ; but it is only an interesting relic of the past which no one can, or ever will, read.

INDIAN SINGING.

1689.   We have the following information
1689. concerning the music in the Indian churches.
A letter,[1] from New England to Her Royal High-
ness, the Princess of Orange, says: " When the
Ruler of the Assembly hath finished his prayer, the
whole congregation of Indians praise God with
singing; in which many of them are excelling."
From this it would seem that they had been
instructed, and that, most likely, by Mr. Elliot.

In 1705, Dr. Increase Mather, Dr. Cotton
1705. Mather, and Rev. Nehemiah Walter, in a
letter to Sir William Ashhurst, speak of the
Indians' " Excellent singing of Psalms, with most
ravishing melody." And again, " that Jonathan
George, (an Indian,) set the tune for the Psalm
and carryed it out most melodiously." In 1687,
a letter from Dr. In. Mather to Dr. John Leusden,
Hebrew professor in the University at Utrecht,
says: " The whole congregation of Indians praise
God with singing, and some of them are excellent
singers."

MUSIC FIRST PRINTED.

About the year 1690, there was for want
1690. of a proper supply of tunes, a general dulness

---

[1] This letter may be seen in the Library of Harvard College.

and monotony in the music of the church. Many congregations had scarcely more than three or four tunes that they could sing. This great scarcity created the necessity of appending music to the Psalm Book, which was done about the year 1690; for Mr. Symmes says in a "Dialogue," printed in 1723: "As to Hackney, or St. Mary's it has been pricked" (printed) "in one edition of our Psalm Books above these thirty years." The edition to which he refers, is probably the first to which music was appended. The first we have been able to find was printed at Boston in 1698. There is no doubt, however, from the ^{1698.} above quotation, that one edition or more in which music was printed, preceded this; and that music was printed in this country, as early as 1690. The printing of the edition of 1698 is badly done, with many errors, and without bars, except to divide the lines of poetry. Under each note is placed the initial of the syllable to be applied in singing by note, with other directions for singing. The tunes are named, Litchfield, Low Dutch or Canterbury, York, Windsor, Cambridge, St. Davids, Martyrs, Hackney or St. Marys; and 100, 115, 119, 148th Psalm Tunes. They are printed in two parts only, and immediately preceding them is found

" SOME FEW DIRECTIONS

for ordering the voice in Setting these following
Tunes of the Psalms.

" First, observe how many notes compass the
tune is.   Next the place of your first note; and
how many notes above and below that ; so as you
may begin the tune of your first note, as the rest
may be sung in the compass of your and the people's voices, without Squeaking above, or Grumb-
ling below.   For the better understanding of
which, take notice of the following directions.

" Of the eight Short Tunes used to four lines
only, whose measure is to eight syllables on the
first line, and six on the next ; and may be sung
to any Psalm of that measure.

> Oxford Tune }
> Litchfield Tune } To Psalms
> Low Dutch Tune } Consolatory.

> York Tune } To psalms of Prayer,
> Windsor Tune } Confession and Funerals.

" Cambridge Short Tune, to peculiar Psas. — as
21, 24, 33, 70, 86 first metre, 114, 132.

" These six short tunes in the tuning the first
note, will bear a cheerful high pitch, in regard to
their whole compass from the lowest note, the
highest is not above five or six notes.

St. Davids Tune ⎱ To Psalms of Praise
Martyrs Tune   ⎰ and Thanksgiving.

" These two tunes are eight notes compass above the first note, and therefore begin the first note low.

" Of five long tunes following.

" Hackney Tune — 119 Psa Tune, second Metre — These two Tunes begin your first note low, for the compass is nine notes, and eight above the first note of the tune.

" 100 Psa. Tune — This one tune begin your note indifferent high, in regard you are to fall four notes lower than your first pitch note.

" 115 Psa. Tune and 148 Psa. Tune — These two tunes, begin your first note low, in regard the tune ascends eight notes above it."

The state of musical knowledge and musical skill was such as to demand these directions. Instruments were not used; and they were utterly without knowledge as to the degree of pitch indicated by the letters. Hence these were the best directions that could be given; and they are copied to show the state of musical knowledge at that time.

STERNHOLD AND HOPKINS.

In 1693 an edition[1] of Sternhold and
1693. Hopkins's version was published at Cambridge, and was used to some extent in the churches. This however, never became a general favorite; yet, in a few instances, it must have been used until near the time of the American Revolution. Its want of conformity to the original was the principal fault urged against it. In this respect it was inferior to either "Ainsworth" or the "New England Version;" but in point of smoothness and rhythm, it was perhaps equal, if not superior to either.

As this was considerably used in the Colonies, and as it was the first complete version of the psalms ever made in English verse, we introduce two psalms as a specimen of its poetry. They are interesting, as a historic reminiscence,[2] and are

[1] The first edition of Sternhold and Hopkins's version consisted of fifty-one psalms, and was published in 1549; and the second, in 1553.

[2] When the unhappy Charles fled from Oxford, he threw
1646. himself upon the army of his countrymen, then encamped before Newark. Here, instead of being befriended, he was reproached and insulted to his face. Upon one occasion during public service, one of the chaplains after having used harsh language, directed to be sung the psalm beginning thus:

> "Why dost thou, Tyrant, boast thyself,
> Thy wicked deeds to praise."

for that reason selected. They also present a specimen of each of the versifier's poetry. The first is by Hopkins and the second by Sternhold. They are selected from a work imprinted " John Day, London, 1583."

" PSLA. LII. I. H."

1. Why dost thou, Tyrant, boast thyself,
    thy wicked deeds to praise,
    Dost thou not know there is a God,
    whose mercies last always?
2. Why doth thy mind yet still deuise
    such wicked wiles to warp?
    Thy tongue untrue, in forging lies
    is like a razor sharp.

3. On mischief why setst thou thy mind
    and wilt not walk upright :
    Thou hast more lust false tales to finde
    then bring the truth to light.
4. Thou doest delight in fraude and guile,
    in mischief bloud and wrong :
    Thy lips have learned the flattering style
    O, false deceitful tongue.

As soon as they had sung it, the king rose and requested the soldiers to sing the psalm,

" Have mercy, Lord, on me I pray,
For men would me devour."

This was accordingly sung in compassion for his distress, — a distress that saw no relief until it was found at the scaffold ordered by the High Court of Justice.

5. Therefore shall God forever confound,
    and plucke thee from thy place :
    Thy seed root out from of the ground,
    and so shall thee deface :
6. The just when they behold thy fall
    with feare wile praise the Lord :
    And in reproach of thee withall
    cry out with one accord.

7. Behold the man which would not take,
    the Lord for his defence :
    But of his goods his God did make,
    and trust his corrupt service.
8. But I an Olive fresh and greene,
    shall spring and spread abroad :
    For why alway my trust hath bene
    upon the living God.

9. For this therefore will I give praise,
    to thee with hart and voyce
    I will set forth thy name always
    wherein thy saints rejoyce.

PSAL. LVI.   T. S.

1. Have mercy, Lord, on me, I pray
    for men would me devour :
    He fighteth with me day by day,
    and troubleth me each houre.
2. Mine enemies daily enterprise,
    to swallow me outright ;
    To fight against me many rise
    O thou most high of might.

3. When they would make me most afraid
    with boasts and brags of pride :
   I trust in thee alone for ayde,
    by thee I wil abide.

4. God's promise I do mind and praise,
    O, Lord I stick to thee :
   I do not care at all afraies,
    what flesh can do to me.

5. What things I either did or spake
    they wrest them at their wil :
   And all the councel that they take,
    is how to work me il.

6. They all consent themselves to hide,
    close watch for me to lay :
   To spie my pathes and snares have tide,
    to take my life away.

7. Shall they thus scape on mischiefe set;
    thou God on them wilt-frown :
   For in his wrath he will not let,
    to throw whole kingdoms down.

8. Thou seest how oft they make me flee
    and on my tears dost looke ;
   Reserve them in a glass by thee
    and write them in thy book.

9. When I do call upon thy name
    my foes away do start :
   I wil perceive it by that same
    that God doth take my part.

10. I glory in the word of God
    to praise it I accord
   With joy I shall declare abroad,
    the promise of the Lord.

11. I trust in God and yet I say
    as I before began :
    The Lord he is my help and stay,
    I do not care for man.

12. I will perform with hart so free,
    to God my vowes always :
    And I O Lord all times to thee,
    will offer thanks and praise.

13. My soul from death thou doest defend,
    and keep my feet upright :
    That I before thee may ascend
    with such as liue in light.

We will give one short Hymn as a specimen of
that style of Poetry.   .

"A SONG TO BEE SUNG BEFORE THE MORNING PRAYER."

1. " Praise yee the Lord yee Gentiles all
    which hath brought you into his light,
    O, praise him all people mortall,
    as it is most worthy and right.

2. " For he is full ditermined,
    on vs to poure out his mercy ;
    And the Lord's truth be yee assured
    abideth perpetually.

Glory be to God the Father,
    and to Iesus Christ his true sonne
With the Holy Ghost in like manner,
    now and at every season."

REV. JOHN TUFTS'S BOOK.

About the year 1712,[1] the Rev. Mr. Tufts, pastor of the Second Church in Newbury, published a musical work, entitled: " *A very plain and easy Introduction to the Art of Singing Psalm Tunes : With the Cantus or Trebles of Twenty-eight Psalm Tunes, contrived in such a manner, as that the Learner may attain the Skill of Singing them, with the greatest ease and Speed imaginable. By Rev. Mr. John Tufts.* Price 6*d.* or 5*s.* the duz.'' Having never seen this work, the writer is unable to give any account of it, or its contents. The only knowledge he has of it, was gained from its advertisement, as was customary in those days, on the blank page of the Rev. **Mr.** Symmes's discourse, " Concerning Prejudice in matters of Religion."

1712.

MR. TUFTS'S SECOND BOOK.

Mr. Tufts also published another work, the title page of which was as follows : " *An Introduction*

---

[1] We are sorry that we cannot give the precise date of this work ; and hope that this, and many other deficiencies may be remedied by those who have the information at hand. We have no doubt that copies of this, and the succeeding work are still extant, and can easily be found by the friends of music.

*to the singing of Psalm-Tunes ; in a plain and
easy method ; With a Collection of Tunes in
three Parts. By the Reverend Mr. Tufts. The
Eleventh edition. Printed from Copper-plates,
neatly engraven. Boston N. E. Printed for
Samuel Gerrish. 1744."*

1714.   This work is supposed to have been published as early as 1712 or 14. We could
hardly expect the editions to come out oftener than
once in three years upon an average. In addition
to this, we have the word of a gentleman, who is
always correct in dates of olden time, that he has
seen a copy of it dated 1714.

The work was prepared to be bound up with
the Bay Psalm Book ; to which was added a
" Supplement containing other Scripture Songs ;
placed in order as in the Bible." Of these there
were fifty-eight pages.

The " Introduction to the Singing of Psalm-
tunes," occupies five entire pages. The whole is
on a new plan, in which *letters* are used upon the
staff instead of *notes*. The letters are the initials
of the names of the notes. Thus F for faw, is
used on *one* and *four* of the scale ; as S for sol, is
used on *two* and *five*. The time was marked by
placing one or more points on the right side of the
letter, " Thus, F: is to be sounded as long as you

would be distinctly telling One, Two, Three, Four.
A letter with but one point (thus F.) is to be
sounded while you are telling One, Two. A letter without a point (thus F) only half as long."
Ex. F: equal to ⊡, F. equal to ⌒, F equal to ⌐·

"When you find two letters tied together with
a bow, (thus F͡S) they are to be sounded no longer
than you would be singing a letter without a point."

But a single example will render it intelligible.

YORK. C. M.

The music was written in three parts only; and
was purely choral, which, at that day, was the only
style used. The collection consisted of thirty-
seven tunes, and all but one was written in common metre. This one, Commandment, is in Long
Metre.

The next effort for the improvement of Psalmody in New England, was in 1718; when
Dr. Cotton Mather published his   1718.

"PSALTERIUM AMERICANUM."

1718. *" The Book of Psalms in a translation exactly conformed unto the Original ; but all in blank verse. Fitted unto the tunes commonly used in the Church."*

This version has an introduction, at once learned, interesting and evangelical. Each psalm is accompanied by illustrations " To assist the Reader in coming at the vast *Profit* and *Pleasure,* which is to be found in this rare part of the Christian *Asceticks,* every PSALM is here *Satellited* with ILLUSTRATIONS, which are not fetched from the *Vulgar Annotations,* (whereof still, Reader, continue thy esteem and thy improvement.)   But are the more Fine, Deep, and *Uncommon Thoughts,* which in a course of long Reading and Thinking have been brought in the way of the Collector.   They are *Golden* Keys to Immense Treasures of *Truth.*"

The Introduction is an essay upon the excellence of the psalms, and the manner of the translation ; and the psalms themselves, a good metrical version, without injuring the conformity to the original, " for the clink of rhyme."   In regard to the exactness of the translation, our author says : " For the *New Translation* of the PSALMS, which is here endeavoured, an *Appeal* may be with much assurance made, unto all that are Masters of the HEBREW TONGUE, whether it be not much more agreeable to the *Original*, than the *Old* one, or than any that has yet been offered unto the World. . . . . It keeps close to the *Original*; and even when a *word of supply* is introduced, it is usually a needless compliment unto the *care of exactness*, to distinguish it at all, as we have done, with an Italic-Character; for it is really in the Intention and Emphasis of the Original. Yea, the just *Laws* of *Translation* had not been at all violated, if a much greater Liberty had been taken, for the beating out of the Golden and Massy *Hebrew* into a more *Extended English* " [1]

It is not a little strange that so good a work should have been doomed to such a fate. We have not learned that it was ever used; while some in rhyme, though far inferior, have met with favor. This, probably, was owing to its being written in blank verse.

It was all arranged in a line of eight, and a line of six syllables,[2] alternate, or in " Common Metre,"

[1] This version has been commended by a good Hebrician for its ; exactness of translation.

[2] The early metrical composures were nearly all in lines of eight and six syllables alternate; hence the name, "Common Metre." When they lengthened the second and fourth lines, they called it " Long Metre;" and when they shortened the first, " Short Metre."

as were nearly all the metrical composures of that time. Some of the psalms were arranged for Long Metre tunes, by putting two conjoint syllables in the second, and in the fourth lines of each stanza, in a black letter. These could either be sung or omitted without injuring the sense. Hence, such psalms could be sung to Long Metre tunes, or by omitting the black letter, to Common Metre. Psalm 136 was so arranged as to change it from Common to *Short* Metre, by omitting the black letter, in the first line.

At this day it would need changing, to smooth its numbers and complete its cadence ; but still, a noble contrast will be seen between the commencement of the Twenty-third psalm in this, and the examples from the other books.

> " My Shepherd is th' Eternal God :
>   I shall not be in want."

As an example of this work, we will give the following psalms.

POETRY OF PSALTERIUM AMERICANUM.

Psalm III.

" *A Psalm of David, when he fled from Absalom his Son.*"

1. ETERNAL GOD, how they're increas'd ‖ who greatly trouble me ? ‖ How many are the men that stand ‖ in triumph over me ? ‖

2. Many there be who ever are ‖ saying unto my Soul, ‖ Ther's no Salvation to be had ‖ for him in God at all. ‖ Selah. ‖

3. But now about me thou'rt a shield, ‖ O thou ETERNAL GOD, ‖ Thou art my Glory, and thou art ‖ th' uplifter of my head. ‖

4. Unto th' ETERNAL God, I cried, ‖ with my extended voice, ‖ And He gave answer unto me ‖ out of His holy hill. ‖ Selah. ‖

5. I laid me down, and took my sleep ; ‖ and then I did awake : ‖ Because that the ETERNAL God ‖ sustain'd me all along. ‖

6. Tho' there should be ten thousands of ‖ those people who do set ‖ themselves against me round about ; ‖ I will not be afraid. ‖

7. ETERNAL, rise ; save me, my God ; ‖ For thou hast smitten all ‖ my Foes on the cheek-bone ; Thou hast ‖ broken the wicked's teeth. ‖

8. Salvation is what does belong ‖ to the ETERNAL God ; ‖ On those that are thy People is ‖ thy benediction still. ‖

" Illustrations on the third Psalm.

" Singer, Now Meditate on the sufferings of thy SAVIOUR. The Fifth Verse evidently mentions His Death and Resurrection. Compare the Third Psalm with the Sixteenth.

" 2. They thought the Crimes of David past Expiation. This is the Jewish gloss upon it. But Old Arnobius invites us to consider this Passage, as fulfill'd in the flouts of the Jews at our dying Saviour. And all the rest as fulfill'd in Him.

" 7. Is here no Allusion to Sampson's Victory ? Was it

not literally fulfill'd in the Deaths of Absalom and of Ahito-
phel !

" 8. What? A Blessing wished for such an ungrateful
People ! Christian, imitate this Goodness ! Compare
Gal. vi. 16.''

PSALM IV.

" *To the chief Musician. On Neginoth. A Psalm of David.*"

1. O Thou God of my righteousness, ‖ hear me when I do
call : ‖ Thou hast enlarg'd me when I was ‖ in troublesome
Restraint. ‖ O be thou gracious unto me, ‖ and O hear thou
my prayer. ‖

2. Ye Sons of Men, how long shall my ‖ Glory be turned
to shame ? ‖ How long will you love vanity ; ‖ and how long
seek a lie ? ‖

3. But know, th' ETERNAL sets apart ‖ the pious for
Himself. ‖ Th' ETERNAL God will hear when I ‖ do call
to Him for help. ‖

4. Be you much mov'd ; but do you not ‖ then any more
offend. ‖ Commune with your own heart upon ‖ your bed
and so be still. ‖

5. Offer the Sacrifices which ‖ belong to righteousness : ‖
And therewith place your confidence ‖ on the ETERNAL
God. ‖

6. Many there be that say, O who ‖ will show us what is
good ! ‖ O thou ETERNAL God do thou ‖ signally over
us, ‖ like as a banner, lift the light ‖ of thy bright countenance. ‖

7. Thou hast bestow'd, *in doing thus* ‖ a joy upon my
heart, ‖ more than the time wherein their Corn ‖ and their
Wine did increase. ‖

8. I will both lay me down in peace, ‖ and I will take my

sleep; ‖ For O ETERNAL, Thou alone ‖ dost make me dwell secure. ‖

We give a part of the 116th Psalm as a specimen of the manner in which several psalms were arranged for singing either in Common or in Long Metre. This method was invented by Richard Baxter; [1] who translated the Psalms into English verse, and arranged a part or all in the manner of the following example.

PSALM CXVI.

1. I'm full of Love : It is because ‖ [of thís] that the ETER-NAL God ‖ hath hearkened now unto my voice; ‖ [and hath] my supplications *heard.* ‖

2. Because that He hath unto me ‖ [kíndlɥ] inclined His gracious Ear; ‖ therefore upon Him I will call ‖ while I have any days [of lífe].

3. The cords of Death surrounded me ‖ and me the [dreadful] pains of Hell ‖ found out; a sad anxiety ‖ I found and sighing [heabɥ] grief. ‖

4. But I did call upon the Name ‖ of the ETERNAL God, [for thís]; ‖ I pray Thee, O ETERNAL God, ‖ Deliver thou my [sínkíng] Soul. ‖

5. Most full of tender clemency ‖ [foreber] is th' ETER-NAL God : Righteous He is too; and our God ‖ is most compassionate [wíthall]. ‖

6. The simple ones th' ETERNAL God ‖ takes into [hís kínd] custody ; ‖ I was brought miserably low, ‖ and then [ít was] He helped me. ‖

---

[1] Author of " The Saint's Rest."

7. O thou my Soul, Do thou return ‖ where 'tis [alone] thou findest rest; ‖ Because that the ETERNAL God ‖ hath well [enough] rewarded thee. ‖

8. Because thou hast from *threatening* Death ‖ [safely] delivered my Soul; ‖ my Eye from tear; my foot from fall ‖ by a thrust given [unto] me. ‖

This work was divided into five books.[1] The *first* extended to the forty-second psalm ; the *second*, to the seventy-third ; the *third*, to the nine-tieth ; the *fourth*, to the one hundred and seventh ; and the *fifth*, to the end. At the close there were sixteen pages of hymns, all scripture subjects, and arranged, like the Psalms, in blank verse. This book had no music appended to it, a circum-stance that was the more strange, inasmuch as it was common to add it to their psalms, and there was at that time, great need of music in the colonial churches. Had it been well supplied with proper music, it might have passed into extensive use during the musical reformation that immediately followed its publication.

WALTER'S SINGING BOOK.

1721.

Three years after the publication of Dr. Mather's Psalms, or in 1721, the fourth sing-

---

[1] The Bay Psalm Book and Ainsworth were divided in the same manner.

ing book published in this country, was edited by
Rev. Thomas Walter, of Roxbury, Mass. Previous
to this, no music had been published in the colonies, except that appended to the Bay Psalm Book.
Mr. Walter's book was a small but neat 12mo.
volume. The music was beautifully engraved ;
and the printing clear and neat. It bore the title
of : *" The Grounds and Rules of Musick explained : Or an Introduction to the Art of
Singing by Note : Fitted to the meanest capaci-
ties. By Thomas Walter, A. M. Recommended by Several Ministers. ' Let everything
that hath breath praise the Lord.' Ps. 150, 6.
Boston : Printed by Benjamin Mecom, at the
new Printing Office near the Town House : for
Thomas Johnstone, in Brattle Street."*

Prefixed to this work was the following

" RECOMMENDATORY PREFACE.

" An ingenious hand having prepared instruc-
tions to direct them that would learn to sing
Psalms after a regular manner : and it being
thought proper that we should signify unto the
Publick some of our Sentiments on this occasion :
We do declare, that we rejoice in *good Helps* for
a beautiful and laudible performance of that holy
Service, wherein we are to glorify God, and edify

one another with the spiritual Songs, wherewith he has enriched us.

" And we would encourage all, more particularly our Young People, to accomplish themselves with Skill to *sing the Songs of the LORD*, according to the *good Rules* of Psalmody : Hoping that the consequence of it will be, that not only the *Assemblies* of *Zion* will *decently and in order* carry on this exercise of piety, but also it will be the more introduced into private Families, and become a part of our *Family-Sacrifice.*

" At the same time we would above all exhort, That the *main concern* of all may be to make it not a meer bodily exercise, but *sing with* Grace in their Hearts, and with Minds attentive to the *Truths* in the PSALMS which they sing, and affected with them, so that in their *Hearts they may make a Melody to the* LORD."

Signed, Boston April 18, 1721.

Peter Thacher	Thomas Foxcraft	Benj. Wadsworth
Joseph Sewell	Samuel Checkley	Benj. Colman
Thomas Prince	Increase Mather	Nathaniel Williams
John Webb	Nehemiah Walter	Nathaniel Hunting.
William Cooper	Joseph Belcher	

Then follow

" *Some brief and very plain* INSTRUCTIONS for singing by NOTE." Also

" Rules for tuning the voice."

This is the first music printed with bars in America. The tunes are composed in three parts only; and are made up of half and whole-notes, (minims and semibreves.) The harmony is full, rich and correct; and the whole style, purely choral.

Mr. Walter's book was noticed in the Boston Gazette of May 8, 1721, and duly announced and advertised in the same periodical on the 17th of July. In April, 1723, the second edition of the work, "Enlarged, Corrected and beautified," was advertised in the Gazette. From this time it went through successive editions for many years, and was probably used until supplanted by the publications of Bayley, Billings and others, that succeeded them. The last edition we have seen was published at Boston in 1764. Whether Mr. Walter's or some other book was used, the style of church music before Billings's day, was that of his book.

The price of Mr. Walter's book was "4s. single; and 42s. per doz. Or bound for 5s. single, and 52s. the doz."

One might almost deem the above-named works a superfluity of music; for singing psalm-tunes, at that day, had not become an amusement among the people. It was used, as it ever ought to be, only as a devotional act. So great was the reverence in which their psalm tunes were held, that the people put off their hats, as they would in prayer, whenever they heard one sung, though not a word were uttered.

Singing in parts was scarcely known, and the ability to sing three or four melodies constituted their whole musical knowledge. Using but few tunes in church, and never singing them for amusement; believing that the few they had were as sacred as the words, and feeling as little disposed to make innovations upon them as upon the text, it will easily be conceived that a small amount of music would be all their wants would demand. These few were repeated over once or twice each Sabbath, until their familiarity in the sanctuary was even greater than the psalms themselves; and the psalms were sung until they became familiar as their household names. In pious families two were sung every day in the week, and on the Lord's day not less than eight, thus repeating each psalm not less than six times a year.

MANNER OF SINGING.

In some churches, being furnished with books, they did not read the psalm line by line, but sang without, though generally it was " lined out."

Their psalms were those of the New England version, and they seldom used a hymn. The psalms were not selected to suit the preacher's subject, but were sung in order; at least this was the custom for one part of the day, and in many congregations it was their constant rule.

The following extract from Dr. Cotton Mather's "Church Discipline, or Methods and Customs in the Churches of New England," will show how the singing was conducted, before the year 1720. The book to which we refer was published at 1720. Boston in 1726.

"The former and larger prayer of the pastor being finished, then (as Tertullian tells us how in his time *Psalmi canuntur*) a Psalm usually succeeds. In some, the assembly being furnished with Psalm-books, they sing without the stop of reading between every line.

"But ordinarily the Psalm is read line after line, by him whom the Pastor desires to do that service; and the people generally sing in such grave tunes, as are most usual in the churches of our nation. Basil thus mentions the order in the primitive churches. First praying, and then singing.

"It is manifest, from Tertullian, that in the primitive churches, the Christians used not only hymns collected out of the Sacred Scriptures, but such as

were conceived and composed by themselves. Socrates mentions the psalms written by Chrysostom ;
and Eusebius the psalms written by Nepos. Nor
was it otherwise in the Bohemian churches, of the
later ages, where they were provided with a *Cantional* of above seven hundred and forty *Sacred
Songs*, besides the *Davidical Psalms*. But the
churches of New England admit not into their
public services, any other than the psalms, hymns
and spiritual songs of the Old and New Testament,
faithfully translated into English metre. No: not
so much as the Te Deum ; an hymn which indeed
is not mentioned by any Author more antient than
the rules which old Benet wrote for his *Monks*,
about the middle of the sixth century. Nor the
song of the *Three Children*, an hymn everywhere
unmentioned until the fourth council of *Toledo*, in
the seventh. In this thing they agree to the act of
the Laodicean Synod, *that no private psalms be
used in the church*. And they almost confine
themselves unto the limitations enjoined by the first
synod of *Bracara : Let nothing be sung in the
church, but the psalms of the Old Testament*.

" And if *Austin* could blame the *Donatists*, for
leaving of the psalms of David, and singing Hymns
of their own invention, it is a point wherein the
churches of New England have not been hitherto

blameable. The private families and companies of the Faithful among them, indeed have sometimes employed what versified portions of Scripture and other devout hymns they find for their edification.

" But when they bless God in their congregations, they keep to such psalms, as a Theodoret mentions as preferable in the judgment of several of the *Antients,* above any others ; that is to say, those in our sacred Psalter, and some other poetical paragraphs of the Sacred Scriptures, versified.

" The first Planters of New England, were not long without a version of the Davidical Psalms, and of several other songs in both Testaments, made by the united endeavours of several persons. In this version the poetry may indeed want refining ; yet the nearness and closeness of the translation to the *Original,* may make some amends for other defects. These holy psalms, by some congregations, are sung over in order as they lie ; (at least in the psalmody for one part of the day ;) and in others, are sung, as the minister singles them out, for to accommodate the subjects, and the designs before him.

" Their way of singing is not with such *disorderly clamours* as were condemned by the old council of Trullo ; but in such grave tunes, as are most used in our nation ; and it may be hoped, not

without some sense of that which Zonaras gives as
the reason of the Trullan Condemnation ; *the singing of psalms is a supplicating of* GOD *himself,
wherein by humble prayer we beg the pardon of
our sins.* Their psalmody is neither set off with
the *delicacies* which *Austin* complained of, nor is
it rendered unseemly by the *exorbitances* we find
rebuked by *Chrysostom.* It has been commended
by strangers as generally *not worse,* than what is
in many other parts of the world ; but rather as
being usually according to *Origen's* expression,
melodiously and agreeably. However, of later
times they have considerably recovered it, and reformed and refined it, from some indecencies, that
by length of time had begun to grow upon it. And
more than a score of tunes are heard Regularly
sung in their Assemblies."

MUSIC NOT CULTIVATED.

We have now come down through one century
of our country's history, gathering up such information as we have been able to find, and at this point,
1721, meet the first direct effort at improving
their church music.

1721.

When the Puritans first came to their wilder-
ness-home, they cultivated music even in their

College. Their songs of praise were conducted with decorum, if not with ability; and a laudable pride, if such can be, inspired them still to improve their purity and excellence. This spirit brought out the New England version of Psalms, a work, as a whole, incomparably better than any version that had preceded it.

But soon after their settlement, the Colonies were disturbed by contentions and party strife. Scarcely had a score of fleet years sped their flight, before errors in doctrine came in to disturb that tranquillity for which they had sought these shores. Troubles came upon troubles in rapid succession. The genius of discord settled upon the land. There was Roger Williams, Anne Hutchinson, the Quakers, and Antinomianism, to trouble their religion; the Pequod, King Philip's, and numerous petty wars with the Indians, to alarm the land. Their charters were several times annulled and restored; and oppressive acts, leading to party strife with insurrection, and twice to open war, were passed. Witchcraft, and a host of smaller evils, came swarming over the land, like the plagues of Egypt. Then, not a trouble came upon England, that was not felt in the Colonies. Every one's thoughts were upon the evils and troubles of the day. It was an age of commotion, both in England and in the Colonies.

Music dwells not in scenes of contention ; she flies the abode of anarchy and confusion, and seeks a home in the land of peace. It is there, and there only, she dispenses her blessings.

The few music-books, that had from time to time found their way into the Colonies, were rapidly decreasing ; and the few they had were unlike. The cultivation of music was neglected, until in the latter part of the seventeenth, and at the commencement of the eighteenth century, the congregations throughout New England were rarely able to sing more than three or four tunes. The knowledge and use of notes too, had so long been neglected, that the few melodies sung, became corrupted, until no two individuals sang them alike. Every melody was " tortured and twisted," (embellished ?) " as every inskillful throat saw fit," until their psalms were uttered in a medley of confused and disorderly noises, rather than in a decorous song. The Rev. Mr. Walter says of their singing, that it sounded " like five hundred different tunes roared out at the same time ; " and so little attention was paid to time, that they were often one or two words apart, producing noises " so hideous and disorderly, as is bad beyond expression." The manner of singing had also become so tedious and drawling, that the same author says, " I myself

have twice in one note paused to take breath."
The Rev. Mr. Symmes says, in his sermon on Regular Singing: " It is with great difficulty that this
part of worship is performed, and with great inde-
cency in some congregations for want of skill.   It
is to be feared, singing must be wholly omitted in
some places, for want of skill, if this art is not
revived."

THE REFORM.

The declining state of music had been so
gradual and imperceptible, that the very con-   1720.
fusion and discord was grateful to their ears ; and
a melody sung in time and tune, was really offen-
sive.   At this stage of affairs, some of the best
men of the day, seeing the need of reform, resolved to set about the work.   This they did ; and
about the year 1720, several excellent and spirited
discourses from the best divines, were published
and scattered among the people.   The pulpit, also,
as it was, and ever *is* its duty, fearlessly called for
a better performance of their songs of praise.   Such
men as the Mathers, Edwards, Stoddard, Symmes,
Dwight, Wise, Walter, Thacher, and Prince, indeed, the best and ablest men of the Colonies,
joined heart and hand in the work of reformation.

One might think, that a duty so obvious and

practical, would find none but friends to its best performance. But it was not so. No sooner had the cry for reform been heard, than it was opposed by a large party in almost every church, and opposed with a virulence of feeling, and tenacity of attachment to their old customs, that seemed to defy their best efforts. Objections were urged even by serious, and on other subjects, well informed persons, which, however trifling and pitiful they may seem to us, were to them important and solemn. The idea of learning to sing by note, or to sing a melody correctly, had something in it little less fearful in itself, or in its effects, than witchcraft and its scenes, through which they had just passed.

Their principal objections were :

1. That it was a new way ; — an unknown tongue.

2. That it was not so melodious as the usual way.

3. That there were so many tunes, one could never learn them.

4. That the new way made disturbance in churches, grieved good men, exasperated them and caused them to behave disorderly.

5. That it was popish.

6. That it would introduce instruments.

7. That the names of the notes were blasphemous.

8. That it was needless, the old way being good enough.

9. That it was only a contrivance to get money.

10. That it required too much time to learn it, made the young disorderly, and kept them from the proper influence of the family, &c. &c.

With divers such weighty reasons, all of which were soberly answered, in a clear and forcible manner, by Rev. Messrs. Symmes, Dwight, Walter, Thacher, Danforth, Mather, Stoddard and others; besides those who fully endorsed   1720–2. the printed discussions of the subject. Among these were names that will be remembered, as long as the early history of our country shall be read.

CASES OF CONSCIENCE.

Beside the answers to the above objections, a tract appeared in 1723, called "Cases of Conscience about singing Psalms, briefly   1723. considered and resolved." This is "An Essay [1] by

---

[1] Mr. Allen, in his book of American Biography, credits this work to the Rev. Solomon Stoddard, of Northampton. And also says that it was published in 1722. The copy in the Massachusetts Historical Library, bears the date of 1723. But it may be a second edition.

several ministers of the Gospel, for the satisfaction of their pious and conscientious bretheren, as to sundry Questions and Cases of Conscience, concerning the singing of Psalms, in the public worship of God, under the present Evangelical constitution of the Church-state.   Offered to their consideration in the Lord.   Printed at the desire of Honorable, Reverend and worthy Persons, to whom it was communicated, in a venerable Council of churches.   January 30, 1722."

Signed by PETER THACHER,
JOHN DANFORTH,
SAM. DANFORTH.

Some of these " Cases of Conscience " were :

" Whether you do believe that singing Psalms, Hymns and Spiritual Songs, is an external part of Divine public worship, to be observed in, and by the assembly of God's people on the Lord's Days, as well as on other occasional meetings of the saints, for the worshipping of God."

" Whether you do believe that singing in the worship of God ought to be done skilfully ? "

" Whether you do believe that skilfulness in singing may ordinarily be gained in the use of outward means, by the blessing of God."

" Is it possible for Fathers of forty years old and

upward to learn to sing by rule. And ought they to attempt at that age to learn." [1]

" Do you believe that it is Lawful and Laudable for us to change the customary way of singing, for a more uniform and regular way of singing the Psalms."

" Whether they who purposely sing a tune different from that which is appointed by the pastor or elder to be sung, are not guilty of acting disorderly, and of taking God's name in vain also, by disturbing the order of the sanctuary."

The above objections and cases of conscience, will give a general idea of the character of the discussion, and the circumstances which produced it. Rarely have a people been more excited on a subject admitting so little difference of opinion. So great was the excitement, that Mr. Symmes says : " A great part of the town [2] has for near half a year, been in a mere flame about it." [3] How long

[1] Under the above heads the subject of natural ability was well discussed, and the people encouraged to make the attempt with the prospect of success.

[2] Bradford, Mass.

[3] The following extract was copied from the New England Courant,* Sept. 16, 1723. " Last week a Council of Churches was held at the South part of Braintree, to regulate the disorders 1723. occasioned by regular singing in that place, Mr. Niles, the minister

* The " New England Courant " was a paper which at that time was published in the name of Benjamin Franklin ; though it belonged to his elder brother, James, who having offended the General Court, was forbidden to publish it. The first paper published in the Doctor's name was issued Feb. 11, 1723.

this excitement continued cannot now be told. In
the year 1720, it was raging like the fire on the
dry prairie ; but by whom, or where it was kindled,
is not known.   It spread, in the fury of its power,
over all the New England Colonies, and burnt for
at least ten years, but to purify and brighten the
churches.   In some it was the glorious harbinger
of a great and powerful outpouring of the HOLY
SPIRIT.   Such was it in Newbury, in Northampton, and in several places near Boston, in which it
was immediately followed by the gracious influences
of the SPIRIT ; and though more remote, it was not
less certain, in many of the New England churches.

THE REASONABLENESS OF REGULAR SINGING.

1720.

The first Essay published on the subject
under discussion, that we have been able to

having suspended seven or eight of the church for persisting in their
singing by rule, contrary, as he apprehended, to the result of a former
Council ; but the suspended bretheren are restored to communion,
their suspension declared unjust, and the congregation ordered to sing
by Rote and by Rule alternately for the satisfaction of both parties."

"Dec. 9th, 1723. We have advice from the South part of Braintree, that on Sunday the first instant, Mr. Niles, the minister of that
place, performed the duties of the day at his dwelling house, among
those of the congregation who are opposers of regular singing. The
regular singers met together at the meeting-house and sent for
Mr. Niles, who refused to come unless they would first promise not
to sing regularly ; whereupon they concluded to edify themselves by
the assistance of one of the Deacons who at their desire prayed with
them, read a sermon, &c.

find, was a sermon written by the Rev. Thomas
Symmes, A. M., D. D., of Bradford, Mass., a man
of talent, of great influence and excellence of
character. He wrote and published two sermons,
and one essay upon the subject. The first published in 1720, was called "The Reasonableness
of Regular Singing." The second, in 1722, was on
"Prejudice in matters of Religion." And the
third, in 1723, was his "Utile Dulci; or Joco-
Serious Dialogue."

The following extract from Mr. Symmes's Reasonableness of Regular Singing, is too important to
be omitted, both as an example of his works, and
also as containing much authentic historical matter.
It is probably the first work that was published
upon the discussions of the day; and though not
as well written as some others, is of the greatest
value for its information. Without it many interesting and important facts would have been lost.

The work bears the following title.

THE REASONABLENESS OF REGULAR SINGING, OR SINGING BY NOTE.

" *In an Essay to revive the true and an-*
cient mode of Singing psalm-tunes accord- 1720.
ing to the pattern of our New England psalm-
books, the Knowledge and practice of which, is

*greatly decayed in most congregations. Writ
by a Minister of the Gospel. Perused by several
ministers in the town and country ; and published with the approbation of all who have read
it.*" This was written by the Rev. Thomas
Symmes of Bradford, Mass. delivered at a singing
meeting in his own parish, also in several other
places, and published in 1720. Mr. Symmes says:

" The following considerations have occasioned
many people to think that the publishing something of the nature of what is here offered, would
be very serviceable viz.

1. " The total neglect of singing psalms by
many serious christians for want of skill in singing
psalm-tunes. There are many who never employ
their tongues in singing God's praises because they
have no skill. It is with great difficulty that this
part of worship is performed, and with great inde-
cency in some congregations for want of skill; It
is to be feared singing must be wholly omitted in
some places for want of skill if this art is not revived. I was once present in a congregation,
when singing was for a whole Sabbath omitted,
for want of a man able to lead the assembly in
singing.

" 2. The imperfect and irregular manner of
singing tunes in most places. Some of the tunes

are varied much, (and much more in some congregations than others,) from the pattern or notes in our own psalm-books and from the rules of music.

"3. The difficulties and oppositions which some congregations have met withal, in their attempting and accomplishing a reformation in their singing. These arose in a great measure, from the misapprehendsions and mistakes, of some honest and well-minded People among them. Thus it has happened in some, though not in all congregations, when singing has been reformed. It is hoped that as the contentions of *Paul* and *Barnabas,* were overrulled for the more effectual spreading of the Gospel; so the oppositions that some have made against *regular singing*, will prove a means for the more speedy and successful reviving of the duty of singing psalms, and that in the most decent, Regular way.

"4. The success which has followed suitable endeavours to remove those cavils which some, (while they labor under their prejudices to singing by Rule,) have thought were unanswerable reasons in their favour. Experience has sufficiently shown, in scores of instances, that the most vehement opposers of singing by note, never fail of being convinced of their mistakes, as soon as they

gain a competent knowledge in the rules of singing, with ability to sing a small number of tunes
with some exactness. I have never known, as I
remember, or heard of one instance to the contrary. The Reasonableness of singing by note
and its excelling the usual way, cannot be fully
understood by any, till they have attained some
skill in the rules of singing; yet there is so much
reason for singing according to note, more than for
the other way, as may satisfy any rational, unprejudiced person, that is much rather to be chosen.

" I shall now proceed in the plainest most easy
and popular way I can, (for it is for the sake of
the common people I write,) to show, *That singing by, or according to note*, is to be preferred to
the *usual way of singing*, which may be evidenced by several arguments.

1. " The first argument may be taken from the
Antiquity of *Regular Singing.* Singing by
note is the most ancient way of singing, and
claims the preference to the other on that account.
Truth is older than Error ; and is venerable for its
antiquity ; but as for Error, the older it is, the
worse it is. There are many bad *Old Ways* —
Antiquity is no infallible mark of Truth. Math.
5. 21. Yet the argument may be of service here,
because those who plead against *singing by rote*,

urge with much zeal and warmth, that this is a *new way*, and the *usual way is the good old way*, as they call it. Here I shall endeavor to prove their mistake ; and I suppose, that if they could be convinced, that singing by note was known to, and approved of, by the first settlers in New England, it would satisfy most of them as to this point ; and if this be not done, it may be some will be so unreasonable as to think the point not made out, though it could be plainly proved to be at an equal date, to that of *Instrumental Music.* It is more than probable, it was known and approved of by the first inhabitants of New England. For,

I. "It was studied, known and approved of in our College, for many years after its first founding. This is evident from the Musical Theses which were formerly printed, and from some writings containing some tunes, with directions for singing by note, as they are now sung; and these are yet in being, though of more than sixty years standing ; besides no man that studied music, as it is treated of by Alstead, Playford and others, could be ignorant of it."

II. "If singing by note was not designed, why were the notes placed in our New England Psalm-books, and some general directions there given about them ?   If they were designed for a pattern for us to sing by, either it was a true and exact pattern or not.   If it was not, either skill or honesty, or both were wanting in our *predecessors*, and surely you will have so great and just a veneration for them, as not to suspect either of these things of them ; but if the pattern was exact and was sang by, then, singing by note is of ancient date with us in this land.

3. " There are many persons of credit now living, children and grand-children of the *first* settlers of New-England, who can very well remember that their Ancestors sung by *note*, and they learned to sing of them, and they have more than their bare words to prove that they speak the truth ; for many of them can sing tunes exactly by note which they learnt of their fathers, and they say that they sang all the tunes after the same manner ; and these people now sing those tunes most agreeable to note, which they have least practiced in the congregation.   But suppose singing by note was not practiced, and that the *usual way* was in our congregations from the first settling of New-England ; it does not therefore follow, that *singing by note*, is not of the antientest date, nor that the usual way of singing is the best.   For I suppose you will grant that there was a *possibility*

of their singing in a way that was not of the most ancient practice among the people of God ; and I will prove that there was *more than a probability* of it, if they sang not by note, but in *your common way :* I will prove it thus ; — That way of singing which all the books that treat of *vocal music,* and especially of *psalm-tunes* describes to be the way which was owned and taught as the true mode of singing, must in all probability be of ancienter date, than that mode or way, which was never so much as mentioned in any one book that treats of singing. Now, all *Treatises of Psalm-tunes,* which I have ever seen or heard of, speak only of singing by note, as the true and proper way of singing *psalm-tunes ;* and if there can be one book produced, which treats of *vocal music,* and gives plain rules for, and commends your usual way of singing, above that of singing according to the notes in our New-England psalm books, then it shall be granted that you have far more reason on your side, than could ever be discovered by any but yourselves.

" *Objection.* But some will say, *If singing by note* is the ancientest way, how came it that it was not continued — when or by whom was it laid aside, or altered ?

" Ans. The declining from, and getting beside

the rule, was *gradual and insensible.* — *Singing Schools* and *Singing books* being laid aside, there was no way to learn ; but only by hearing of tunes sung, or by taking the *run of the tune,* as it is phrased. The rules of singing not being taught or learnt, every one sang as best pleased himself, and every *leading-singer,* would take the liberty of raising any note of the tune, or lowering of it, as best pleased his ear; and add such *turns* and *flourishes* as were grateful to him ; and this was done so gradually, as that but few if any took notice of it. One *Clerk* or *Choirister* would alter the tunes a little in his day, the next a little in his, and so one after another, till in *fifty* or *sixty* years it caused a considerable alteration. If the altera-tion had been made designedly by any *Master* of *Music* it is probable that the variation from our *psalm-books* would have been alike in all our con-gregations ; whereas some vary much more than others, and it is hard to find *two* that sing *exactly alike.* The alteration being so *gradual,* it is no wonder that people are ignorant when it was made, or that there is any at all. As *weights* and *measures,* which are sealed, with using them *seven* or *ten* years, may alter considerably, and the per-son using them not discern it, till he compares them with the *standard,* and then he is presently convinced of it. We are well informed, that in other countries where *Singing Schools* are kept up, singing is continued in the purity of it: Where they are not it is degenerated as it is among us. Your *usual way* of singing is handed down by *tradition* only, and whatsoever is only so conveyed down to us, it is a thousand to one if it be not miserably corrupted, in *three* or *four-score* year's time." . . . . .

In the following, as well as some of the foregoing extracts, the reader will find too much history, to complain of its length. Some of these extracts have been made almost exclusively to show, in the language of the day, the state of feeling on these subjects. Others have been taken, to show the peculiar character of the discussions.

III. " *That way of singing which is most* RATIONAL *is the best and most excellent ;* but singing by note *is the most rational way,* therefore it is the *most excellent.* Singing by note is singing according to rule, but the usual way of singing is not so, any further than it agrees with singing by note, and *so far* there is no controversy about it. Singing is as truly an art or science, as Arithmetic, Geometry &c. It has certain and plain rules by which it is taught, and without conforming to *them,* there is no true singing. There is a reason to be given why each note in a tune, is placed where it is, *why* and *where* every turn of the voice should be made, how *long* each note should be sung &c. Now singing by note is giving every note its proper *pitch*, and *turning* the voice in its proper place, and giving to every note its true *length* and *sound* &c. Whereas the usual way varies much from this. In it some notes are sung too *high*, others too *low*, and most too *long*, and many *turnings of*, or *flourishes with* the voice, (as they call them) are made where they should not be, and some are wanting where they should have been: All contrary to the rules of singing and create an *ungrateful jarr* in the ears of those who can well distinguish sounds, and have real skill in the rules of singing.

"It is most rational in any art or Science to practice according to the rules of it, especially in that which is used in the joint worship of God; where every man is following his own *fancy*, and leaving the *rule* is an inlet to great confusion and disorder, which is very contrary to Him who is not the *Author of confusion*, but the GOD of *Order*, as in all the Churches of the saints. . . . .

IIII. "*If skill by note is most agreeable to Scripture precept and pattern, then it is better than the vulgar or usual way; but singing by note or by rule is so;* Therefore, singing with *skill* or by *note* which is the same thing, is most agreeable to the general instructions which we have in scripture, about the *external* part of singing. Singing by note agrees best with that direction, *play skillfully* Ps. 33, 3. There is as much reason why we should sing skilfully in God's worship, as there was for the Jews *playing skillfully.* It was written for *our* as well as *their* instruction. Skill in any art or science implies a knowledge of, and conformity to the rules of it ; which they have not who plead for and sing in the usual way. A parrot can imitate us in many words and sentences, yet has not skill or understanding in speaking. . . . . .

" Thus have I shown that singing by note is the *most ancient, melodious and rational way and most agreeable to scripture precept and pattern.* Much more might be said in favour of regular singing, as that, it is most *grave* and *decent*, and best answers the end of singing every way. And it is not without reason that regular singing most resembles the singing which will be the employment of Saints and Angels in the *heavenly world*, of any singing on Earth. And what follows is an argument of no little weight in it ; it would give regular singing the preference, if they were equal for *age*, *melody, reasonableness,* and *agreement with Scripture precept and pattern.*"

The following brief extract from the same Essay is worthy of particular notice. The writer believed that *all* could learn to sing; and so did many others, who were engaged in that great reformation. As they believed all had the ability to learn, so they enjoined the duty upon *all.* Mr. Symmes says p. 14.

"If all in this Province who can never learn one tune in the usual way, would industriously apply themselves to learn to sing by note, and in order to that, furnish themselves with *Singing-books,* and go to a *Skilfull Singer* for instructions, it is thought by a very moderate computation, that in one year's time, more than *Ten-thousand* persons might learn to sing *psalm-tunes,* with considerable *skill* and *exactness;* and of the *rising generation* yearly more than a Thousand. And it is not a little thing to have so many voices employed in singing God's praises skilfully in the public, and to have *Thousands* of families enabled to practice this duty in their houses, who now omit it for want of skill." [1]

[1] Upon this subject we find further testimony in a work called "Cases of Conscience" about singing of Psalms briefly considered and resolved," which is introduced at this place for its testimony on this subject. The writers say :

The clergy at this time, saw the necessity, and strongly urged the duty of learning to sing. To this end they warmly advocated the necessity of establishing singing schools. Mr. Symmes says on this subject:

" Would it not greatly tend to promote singing of psalms if singing schools were promoted? Would not this be a conforming to *scripture pattern?* Have we not as much need of them as God's people of old? Have we any reason to expect to be inspired with the gift of singing, any more than that of *reading?* Or to attain it without suitable means, any more than they of old, when *miracles, inspirations* &c. were common? Where would be the *difficulty,* or what the *disadvantages,* if people who want skill in singing, would procure a *skilfull person* to *instruct* them, and meet two or three evenings in the week, from *five* or *six* o'clock to *eight,* and spend the time in

---

"Skilfulness in singing psalms is an acquired gift; and many thousands have attained it, by the *Divine Blessing* on their reading and hearing of the rules of singing, and minding and conforming to the voices of good singers, and to their manner of singing. Some have a natural genius for it more than others; and some have a natural sweetness and strength of voice above others; yet, there are but few so deaf, dumb, weak and dull, as to be utterly unable to form variety of sounds, and to distinguish of *tones* and tunes, and so be incapacitated to receive instruction for the musical and melodious singing of psalms." See p. 3.

learning to sing? Would not this be an innocent and profitable *recreation*, and would it not have a tendency, if prudently managed, to prevent the unprofitable expense of time on other occasions? Has it not a tendency to divert young people, who are most proper to learn, from learning *idle, foolish*, yea, *pernicious songs and ballads*, and banish all such *trash* from their minds? Experience proves this. Would it not be proper for *school masters* in *country parishes* to teach their *scholars*? Are not they very unwise who plead against learning to sing by rule, when they cant learn to sing at all, unless they learn by rule? Has not the grand enemy of souls a hand in this who prejudices them against the best means of singing?

" Will it not be very servicible in ministers to encourage their people to learn to sing? Are they not under some obligations by virtue of their office so to do? Would there not, at least in some places, appear more of that fear of man, which brings a snare, than of true christian prudence in omitting this? And as circumstances may allow, would it not be very useful and profitable if such ministers as are capable, would instruct their people in this art? "

After this, several works appeared, written by some of the best men in the colonies. This, no doubt, is an evidence of the universality of the feeling on this subject. If the clergy, and the best clergy in the colonies, deemed it of sufficient value, thus deeply to interest them, certainly the people, whom it affected more, would not feel it less.

The next Essay that appeared, in order — so far as we have found — was Dr. Cotton Mather's

"ACCOMPLISHED SINGER."

This was published at Boston in 1721. Like most of his works it is full of good thought and right feeling, but abounds more in historic fact, and classical allusion. It is entitled: *" The Accomplished Singer. Instructions how the Piety of Singing with a true devotion, may be obtained and expressed ; the* GLORIOUS GOD *after an uncommon manner Glorified in it, and his people edified.*

" Intended for the assistance of all that sing psalms with grace in their hearts : but more particularly to accompany the laudable endeavours of those who are learning to sing by Rule, and seeking to preserve a REGULAR SINGING *in the Assemblies of the Faithful."*

This Essay commences with the following

"PROPOSAL."

"It is proposed that the pastors of the Churches, would frequently use, a short expository Preface, (which need not extend beyond four or five minutes,) upon that paragraph of a Psalm, which is going to be sung in the Congregation : A short *Exposition* expressing the *Lessons* of PIETY to be found in the verses now to be sung, and the *tempers* or *wishes* of PIETY, which they are to be sung withal. What a marvellous improvement in piety ; yea, what a concert with the *Multitude of the Heavenly Host*, would there follow, upon such a proposal duly prosecuted ! "

This work ought to be introduced entire ; but we have only room for two short extracts. It designs to show, that we *ought* to sing ; and *how*, and *what* we ought to sing. Under the head that we *ought* to sing he urges that " singing is *natural* worship ; " and that it is a *"positive institution of God."* We will here make one short extract relating to *what* we should sing. It is quite as applicable now, as then.

1721.   " The songs which are prepared for us by the Holy Spirit of God, in the inspired writings, that shine in this dark place, ought certainly to be preferred with us, before any mere human composures, in the public worship of the faithful. Those which for their original are peculiarly the songs of Zion, are the most proper to be used in its assemblies. It is true devout hymns composed by the good men of our own time, affected with the *Truths* of God, and able to handle the pen of the writer, for soaring poetry, may be used, and found good for the use of edifying. From Tertullian we learn that in his early days the *Christians* used even such hymns as were conceived by themselves. Socrates mentions the psalms written by Chrysostom, and Eusebius mentions the psalms written by Nepos. The Arians made many hymns to be sung for the propagation of their *heresies ;* and the Orthodox willing to be made wise by their enemies, made hymns for the Preservation of the faith once delivered to the Saints. Yea, great was the army of them who followed Ambrose in publishing of hymns for the use of the Latin Church. The Te Deum ascribed unto Ambrose, makes to this day a mighty noise in the world. The German Psalter has in it hymns of Luther's composing. And in the Bohemian Churches of the later days, they had a Cantional, in which there were seven hundred and forty sacred songs, besides the Davidical Psalms. But certainly, the hymns of uninspired men, cannot be so profitable for all Instruction in Righteousness, and may not have so much respect paid unto them, as those that are given by Inspiration of God.   Austin did well to blame the Donatists for leaving the psalms of David and singing hymns of their own invention.   Yea, if the limitations ordered by a Synod at Bracara, were perhaps a little too strict, yet it was a wise order passed in a Synod at Laodicea, that forbad private psalms to be used in the Church.   The French Churches have wisely confined themselves unto the Scripture Songs ; and the Dutch have harmonized with them.   Can anything be so rich, so full, so sublime, as what the holy spirit of God has declared ?   Every line will weigh against a golden wedge of Ophir ; every word is a pearl, and has a sense and worth in it that is invaluable.   The psalms of David were sung in Jehosaphat's time, as he commanded the Levites to sing praise unto the Lord with the words of David and of Asaph. Words of an excellency, and efficacy, which are not found but where the Spirit of the Lord speaks by men, and his word is in their tongue.   Yea, even the Song of the Lamb, in the fifteenth of the Revelation, seems to be fetched out of the Eighty-sixth psalm ; and the Song of the Angels in the Second of Luke, seems to be fetched out of our

Eighty-fifth. And our blessed Saviour himself, a greater than David, and his Antitype, no doubt, at the Passover, as often as it recurred, sung at least a part of what they called *The Great Hallel,* which was the Hundred and thirteenth psalm, with the five that followed it. In a word we are so directed, Eph. 5, 19. Speak to yourselves in psalms, hymns and spiritual songs. In this direction, there appears an evident reference unto the distinction of the poems in our Hebrew Psalter. The poems are distinguished by three terms, exactly answering unto these. It seems to say, *Let your Psalter supply you with the songs wherein the Admonitions of piety are to be received and preserved and applied among you.*"

The following extract is from the close of the book ; and is selected as a historic record, and as showing the feeling and sentiments of the most influential Minister in the Colonies, upon the subjects then under discussion. He was one of the foremost, as well as one of the ablest, in the cause of musical reform. And it is a fact worth noticing, that the reform was taken up and carried on to its final completion by the Clergy, and by the most influential of the Clergy of the Colonies.

" It is remarkable," says he, " that when the kingdom of God has been making any new appearance, a mighty zeal for the singing of psalms has attended it, and assisted it.   And may we see our people grow more zealous of this *good work ;* what a hopeful sign of the times would be seen in it, ' that *the time of singing has come, and the voice of the Turtle is heard in our land.*'

   " But in the pursuance of this holy intention, it would be very desirable, that people (and especially our young people who are most in the years of discipline,) would more generally learn to sing, and become able to *sing* by *rule,* and keep to the *notes* of the *tunes,* which our spiritual songs are set unto ; which would be to sing agreeably and melodiously. In early days a famous Council condemned it, in that there were *disorderly clamors,* with which the psalmody was then sometimes disturbed.   In later days Cassander upbraided it — *they made bad work of it.*

   " It has been found accordingly in some of our congregations, that in length of time, their singing has degenerated into an *odd noise,* that has had more of what we want a name for, than any ' Regular Singing' in it ; whereby the *celestial exercise* is dishonored ; and indeed the *Third Commandment is trespassed on.*   To take notice of the *ridiculous pleas,* wherewith some very weak people, go to confirm this degeneracy, would indeed be to pay too much respect unto them. And they must have strange notions of the DIVINE SPIRIT, and of his operations, who shall imagine, that the delight which their *untuned ears* take in an *uncouth noise*, more than in *Regular Singing*, is any communion with Him. The skill of *Regular Singing*, is among the gifts of God unto the children of men, and by no means unthankfully to be neglected or despised. For the congregations wherein it is wanting to recover a *Regular Singing*, would be really a *Reformation ;* and a recovery out of Apostacy, and what we may judge that Heaven would be pleased withal. We ought certainly to serve our GOD with the *best*, and *Regular* Singing must needs be better than the confused noise of a *Wilderness*. God is not for confusion in the Churches of his Saints ; but requires, *Let all things be done decently*. It is a great mistake for some weak people, that the tunes regulated with the notes used in the *Regular Singing* of our churches are the same that are used in the Church of Rome. And what if they were ? Our psalms too are used there. But the tunes used in the *French psalmody* and from them in the Dutch also, were set by a famous *Martyr* of JESUS CHRIST ; and when Sternhold and Hopkins illuminated England, with their version of the

psalms, the tunes have been set by such, as good
Protestants may be willing to hold communion
withal. The tunes commonly used in our churches
are *few ;* it were well if they were more.   But they
are also grave, and such as well *become the Ora-
cles of God.* . . . .

    " It is to be desired, that we may see in the
rising generation, a fresh and strong disposition to
learn the proper *tunes ;* that God may be glorified,
and religion beautified, with a Regular Singing
among us ; and that *to them who are his servants,
He may let His work be seen ; His glory also
unto those that are his children here ; and that
the lovely brightness of the Lord who is our* GOD,
*may with conspicuous lustre be seen shining
upon us.*"

        PREJUDICE IN MATTERS OF RELIGION.

           In 1722, a discourse was published " *Con-*
1722.   *cerning Prejudice in matters of Religion. Or
an essay to show the Nature, Causes and Effects
of such Prejudices : And also the means of removing them. By Thomas Symmes, A. M. &c.*"
This discourse was written, and preached at different places ; and was published at the request of
several clergymen who heard it at the Second
Church in Newbury.   Although the words " music "

and " singing " do not once occur in it, yet it was aimed at, and to use the words of the preface, " occasioned by, a most unhappy and unreasonable controversy about singing by note." It is a sound argument, leaving the people without excuse. The text was, John 1, 46. " And Nathaniel said unto him, Can there any good thing come out of Nazareth ? Philip saith unto him, Come and see." The principal points of the discourse were founded on the words " Come and see." In this he urged the wisdom of examining and testing a subject before we condemn it. As this does not touch directly upon the musical history of the times, we will copy nothing from the work.

If reformers were ever guiltless for urging their schemes upon a people, surely these were. The ignorance of the people, and the abuse of this part of divine worship, were excuses enough. Their singing must have been past all endurance, for every one who had the least sensibility or knowledge of the subject. A part of two or three different tunes would be sung to the same stanza ; and sometimes they would be singing different tunes at the same time. The introduction of a new tune, was an event that half centuries saw not — an event that called for the grave decision of the whole church, and sometimes for the parish vote.

The proper manner of introducing a new tune was the grave subject of long and spirited debates, even against the decision of the "Platform of Church Discipline."

So great was the excitement, so earnest the contention, so bitter the animosity, and so dangerous the party feuds, that in 1723, December 23d, "A Pacificatory Letter" was printed and circulated with a view to soothe and calm the commotion of the public mind. This was undoubtedly by Dr. Cotton Mather, and probably, was like oil poured upon the troubled waters. It exhorted to forbearance and long-suffering in both parties, but decidedly favored the reformation. The following are a few extracts from the

1723.

"PACIFICATORY LETTER."

He urges,

1. "That the singing of Psalms is a religious duty incumbent on christians," and proves it by scripture only.

2. "In singing of Psalms regard should be had to something internal, and something external." The heart, and the voice.

3. "In singing, the voice should be governed by rule and measure."

4. "These rules and measures for governing

the voice in singing are not of immediate, divine institution, but the products of human art and skill. Ministers are commanded to preach the word, the Gospel, but they are not directed what particular words and expressions they should use."

5. " Tunes whether new or old are variable."

6. " *Christians should learn to sing Psalms.* Inasmuch as this is a part of religious worship which God requires of his people, they should endeavour to be suitably qualified to manage their part in it."

7. " Where a congregation have sung decently and orderly, yet in length of time, through negligence, and not observing of rules, they may possibly grow very defective in their Psalmody, *and greatly need to amend it.* I dont suppose that the present way of singing in many congregations, is really the old way ; but they have gradually and insensibly varied from that, through want of skill, good heed and observation."

8. " Such amendment may be made, by singing the tunes in common use according to the former rules and measures prescribed for them, or by introducing new tunes, or by singing sometimes the old and sometimes the new."

9. " The same tunes should be usually sung in all our congregations."

10. " Though what is mentioned under the preceeding head, is desirable for the reasons there given ; yet it is far from being *absolutely necessary*."

11. " Different tunes being the product of human art and skill, I see no reason why persons should assume, and impose upon one another the singing of these or those tunes, whether new or old, rather than others."

12. " All tunes being in their own nature indifferent and variable, it seems a pity and shame that any should set up their own wills, be humoursome, contentious, quarrelsome in preferring some of these before others. One would think there might be different apprehendsions about tunes without having fierce contentions in the case. In these things, *agreement* should be peaceably and calmly endeavored.

" Love, Unity, Peace among Christians, are very weighty, important, necessary, indispensible duties plainly and frequently enjoined by the great God our Saviour and our Judge. Endeavoring to keep the Unity of the Spirit in the bond of Peace. Eph. 4. 3. Let love be without dissimulation. Be kindly affectioned one to another, with brotherly love, in honor prefering one another. If it be possible, as much as in you lieth, live peaceably with all men. 2 Cor. 13. 11. Be of one mind, live in peace, and the God of love and peace shall be with you." . . . . . .

"Are we not agreed in the object of our worship, viz. God in Christ Jesus? And in the rule of our religion viz. the Holy Scriptures? And in the translation of the Psalms and Spiritual Songs, and in the Metre commonly used? And being agreed in so many weighty matters, shall we quarrel about what tunes the Psalms shall be sung in? How weak and childish, how foolish, sinful, wicked is this! Shall we that wear the name of *christians*, disobey Christ, that blessed Prince of Peace, grieve his Holy Spirit, dishonor our profession, scandalize our neighbors, make ourselves a scoff and reproach among our enemies, weaken the general interests of piety, break the comfort of our families and churches, and gratify the Devil that worst enemy of God and man, and all this, because of some different apprehendsions about tunes? *O, tell it not in Gath, publish it not in the streets of Askelon!* O, let us study self-denial, mutual forbearance and condescension; and not be humoursome, willful, stiff, resolved in urging our own opinions about tunes, which are in their own nature indifferent and variable. Let us strive against self-conceitedness, not to think too meanly of others, or too highly of ourselves, as though we were the best and wisest and fittest to lead and guide others in these indifferent things."

13. "Those fond of old tunes, should not be too stiff and willful in their own opinions. What, are you so well accomplished, so perfect, as to have no need to learn or amend? Are you so well already, that it is impossible to change or alter your way of singing in any way for the better? Can you be thus conceited of your own attainments? Did you take more pains to learn formerly, than others have done lately? Or can you do better without taking pains to learn, than others with? Pray, do not think too highly of yourselves, nor too meanly of others.

"Dont censure *new singers*, (as they are called) as though they were innovators in God's worship, introducers of indifferent things, or imposers of human inventions. . . . . . . As for an *old* tune, or a *new* one, there is no more *Divinity* in the one than in the other. It is said, those fond of new tunes, are for bringing indifferent things into the worship of God; it may be equally said, those fond of old tunes are for *continuing* indifferent things in the worship of God. But how weak and groundless are charges against one another on such grounds as these? If you say, the most that

are for new singing, (as it is called) are generally
of the younger sort of people ; what then ?   If
they are willing to take pains and learn, that they
may be better able to worship God by singing
Psalms, would you discourage them from this ?
Some have no skill in tunes and singing ; and if
none. at all had, what would become of one part
of God's worship, viz. *the singing of Psalms ?*
Would you have the singing of Psalms continued ?
Doubtless you would ; I am sure you should desire
its continuance.   Well, they cant be sung without
tunes, and if they be not learnt in some measure,
how can they be observed or kept in singing ?
It was the commendation of *Chenaniah,* chief of
the Levites, that *he instructed about song because
he was skillful.* 1 Cron. 15. 22.   If it is commendable to have skill for instructing in the singing of God's praise, then it must be commendable
in others to learn, even to receive such instruction.
If you are fond of old tunes, endeavour to sing
them by note and rule, as much as may be, else
how is it possible that all should agree in any certainty of the tune.   And be not against learning
the new.   I think you should be glad when persons are desirous to learn the singing of Psalms
regularly ; and especially when the younger persons are so, *that one generation may praise God's*

works to another. Dont envy them the skill they
have or desire to attain, in singing Psalms; but
rather countenance, incourage, and promote it as
much as you can.   Phil. 4. 8.   Finally bretheren,
whatsoever things are true, whatsoever things are
honest, whatsoever things are just, whatsoever
things are pure, whatsoever things are lovely, whatsoever things are of good report; if there be any
virtue, if there be any praise, think on these
things.

14. " Those fond of new tunes should not be
vainly or proudly conceited of their own skill or
attainments.   Have you attained more skill in
tunes and in singing than some others?   Then be
thankful for, but not proud of, your Attainments.
You may possibly think you have more skill than
others, when you really have not; and then you
do but flatter and deceive yourselves with a false
notion.   But if you really have attained more
skill than others, in knowing and keeping tune,
and governing your voices; yet, do not think
yourselves such able reformers, as though all were
obliged to follow your opinion and practice.
What rule or authority have you to impose your
own way on others?   If *you* like one tune, may
not *they* as well like another?   If you would not
have them impose by keeping you to the old tunes,

dont you impose by forcing the new on them. If you would personally learn to sing by note and rule, and teach the same to your families, and practice it in some private societies, where the matter is voluntarily come into, I think it is commendable ; but as to the public, you should look on yourselves but as members of the whole : and all members should be more concerned for the good of the whole, than of any particular part. . . . . . . If a number of *new singers* (as some call them) should force in their new tunes into public, without previous leave, consent, or proper and prudent steps to prepare for it ; to the offence, grief and disturbance of the greater part of the people, and it may be the elder and graver part of them ; I believe in so doing they would greatly provoke God, by breaking his command, which requires that *all things should be done to edifying. Learn as fast as you will, excel as much as you can ; yet, be gentle, easy, calm, patient ;* dont force in your new tunes (or method,) till you can do it with public peace." . . . .

" As for regular singing, (so called), I wish it were better understood and practiced through the land ; but as for you who so eagerly endeavor to promote it, are you as properly concerned, about

8

things of equal if not superior weight? Are you as much concerned about the temper of your souls, as the governing of your voice in singing? You do much at singing, what do you at repenting of sin, believing in Christ, sincerely praying to, and obeying of God? If your souls are not uprightly engaged in these duties, the most regular singing you can pretend to, can never bring your soul to Heaven."

1725.   In 1725, a pamphlet was published at Boston, entitled: "An Essay to silence the Outcry that has been made in some places against regular singing, in a sermon preached at Framingham. By the Rev. Mr. Josiah Dwight, Pastor of the Church of Christ in Woodstock. Acts 17, 6. 'These that have turned the world upside down are come hither also.'"

1725.   In the same year, written by the Rev. Valentine Wightman, and dated, Groton, May 20, 1725, was published; "A LETTER to the Elders and brethren of the baptized churches in Rhode Island, Narrhagansit, Providence and Swansy, and the Branches dependent in places adjacent. The love of the FATHER and the righteousness of CHRIST His well BELOVED SON, and comforts of the HOLY SPIRIT be with you all. Amen.

" Beloved Bretheren ;

               " I am under some concern to
write a plea for a long neglected ordinance, to wit,
That of *singing Psalms, Hymns* or *Spiritual
Songs ;* and therefore in order thereunto, I shall
(God assisting) *First* Prove singing of Psalms
Hymns or Spiritual Songs to be the duty of Gen-
tile believers under the Gospel.

" Secondly.   That it is a Moral duty.

" Thirdly.   What singing is.

" Fourthly.   How it ought to be performed.

" And I propose to answer the objections as met
with by the way."

The matter of discussion in these has nearly all
been given in the former extracts ; it is here only
in another dress with some new arrangements ;
we therefore omit any selections from either.

MR. CHAUNCEY'S SERMON.

In 1727, the discussion upon regular singing, had, in all its virulence, extended to 1727.
Connecticut ; and we find an excellent essay, upon
" Singing the Songs of the Lord," by the Rev.
Nathaniel Chauncey, M. A., of Durham, Ct., accepted and adopted, by a General Association of
the clergy, as their sentiments in the following
words :

" This Association having heard the Rev. Mr. Chauncey's arguments for Regular Singing do approve of them and vote them to be printed; recommending them to the public, hoping they may be of Usefulness. As Attests,

" T. Woodbridge, Moderator."

This recommendation was printed on the inside of the title page, in letters so large as to occupy the whole. The Essay was entitled " Regular Singing defended and proved to be the only true way of singing the songs of the Lord; by arguments both from reason and Scripture; Having been heard and approved of, by the General Association at Hartford, May 12, 1727, with their recommendation of it to the public. By Nathaniel Chauncey, A. M.

" II. Cor. 13, 8. We can do nothing against the truth, but for the truth.

" John 8, 46. And if I say the truth why do you not believe me ? — New London. Printed and sold by T. Green, 1728."

Mr. Chauncey's introduction is both able and interesting; and, though worthy of a place, for want of room, it must be omitted. The following extract, though rather long, contains too much both of history and argument to allow an abbreviation. He says:

" The matter of controversy about the performance of this part of Divine Worship, 1727. is this, viz.

" *Whether in singing the Songs of the* LORD, *we ought to proceed by a certain Rule, or to do it in any loose, defective, irregular way, that this, or that people, have accustomed themselves unto?*

" It is a matter the wisest and most able to judge, are clear and full in, and do assert, That there is a certain rule to be used in singing; and it is as clearly discerned, by the best of judges, that this excellent rule is left, and that there are many ill fruits and effects that follow upon the neglect of this rule, or deviation from it.

" Hence it is that a multitude of persons live in a neglect of this duty. Many neglect it in public, they open not their mouths[1] to praise God. And probably many more neglect it in their families and because they know not how to sing.

" Again. For want of knowledge and skill in music, persons cannot have that love for, that delight in, and that relish of the duty, as if they were skilled and did use their skill. This is known to be a truth by the experience of such as once were

---

[1] The Puritans and their children, believed, like the Scotch, that *singing* was a solemn duty, obligatory upon *all*. They sang not by proxy, nor only in church, but in their families.

ignorant and have afterward gotten knowledge. And the truth of this may be seen in other things. The ingenious Artist has much more of pleasure, in his science or trade, than another man who has no skill in it.

" The rule being neglected as useless, the performance is very mean compared with what it would be, were the procedure by rule. It is as flat drink compared with that which is lively, brisk and full of spirit. And the esteem of it is much sunk, and a careless spirit prevails about the performance. And as it has been an unhappiness attending our defective, loose way of doing, that we have been under disadvantages either to discover our defectiveness, or to reform it ; so now, though we are delivered from that, as great, if not a worse evil is met with ; and that is, that having been long accustomed to a loose, irregular way, we are now grown in love with it, and are so far from any willingness to reform, that we cannot bear to have any fault found with our doings in this part of Divine Worship. Many are found so under the influence and power of custom, that they account the common performance to be better, than any reformation can make it ; and are therefore, so far from hearkening to any proposals for a reformation, that the proposal meets with not only rejection, but very fierce opposition, and abundance of censure and reflection ; and some are ready to lavish away as much zeal, as though there were an attempt to pluck away a fundamental article in religion, or to bring in one of the greatest heresies or distructive corruptions into the church. The observation of this is matter of discouragement to attempt to do any service to religion as to this affair. However, there are some considerations that may, notwithstanding, move a man to adventure.

" 1. It is not only the most rational way of treating our fellow creatures to offer plain arguments for their conviction, but it is a thing that is really owing and due unto them.

" 2. It is an honor due to truth. Indeed our zeal is to be wisely and duely proportioned. Our greatest zeal should be about the weightiest points in religion, but smaller things are not to be neglected. But just so much zeal is to be proportioned out unto them as is due. Math. 23, 23. These things ought ye to have done, and not to leave the other undone.

" 3. Such an attempt may do some good, and it may be more than is feared.   But

" 4. In case persons will continue to reject the truth after it has been sufficiently evidenced and proved, and their objections answered, it will make a full discovery of these persons and of the cause of their continuing to oppose and reject the truth. Men's fair pretences will not hide them in so plain a case.

" And this will leave such persons without excuse. John 15. 22. If I had not come and spoken unto them, they had not had sin, but now they have no cloak —— . And this will roll all the blame that comes herefrom at their door — let them use as much subtlety as they have, to shift it off.

" I shall accordingly proceed to make some attempt for the convincing and satisfying of such as reject and oppose the making use of a certain rule in singing. Only I shall premise three things, which I conclude every one will readily concede and grant, that does oppose and withstand the use of a certain rule in singing.

" 1. You grant and readily profess, that you are willing to comply with the mind of God about this matter, if you could but come to the knowledge of it. Every one that dissents professes this. See that there be such an heart in you.

" 2. You will surely grant also that it is a very great sin for men to reject any truth or part of God's mind, in case it comes with due evidence and proof. It is a greater sin than men commonly imagine. And then,

" 3. You will certainly grant that so much proof and evidence as is accounted sufficient and vested in, in other cases and such as are more weighty, should be accounted sufficient in this case. No solid reason can be rendered why more proof and evidence is needful in this matter, than in many points that are more weighty.

" These things being premised, I proceed to lay down the *Assertion* to be made evident. viz.

" *That there is* ONE AND ONLY ONE *sure and certain* RULE *to proceed by, in singing the songs of the* LORD ; *so much knowledge of which, as is needful to the due performance of this part of Divine Service, it is the duty of all, who are to bear a part in singing of those songs, to attain.*"

To illustrate this position, is the great aim of this tract ; and this he does with a power and aptness not often obtained. The whole forms a very powerful and complete argument. Some of his leading ideas in illustrating this are these :

" It is not consistent with the wisdom of God to leave the performance of this duty without a rule to guide it so as to reach these ends.".

" The command to sing involves and includes the rule.

" There is but one instrument that is fit for doing this work.

" The end and design of God's bestowing the gift of Music.

" The scripture precept and example.

" The impossibility of union and good effect in singing without it.

" The ends to be obtained are lost without it.

" There can be no *certain end* without a *certain rule*.

" There must be a certain rule, to judge of the work or duty done.

" There must be a certain rule, to rectify anything amiss.

" There can be neither well-doing nor ill-doing, without a rule.

" There can be no skill.

" If there be no rule, then men have an advantage put into their hands to affront the Majesty of Heaven without trespass or offence.

" If there be no rule, there can be no singing."

His last argument was from testimony, and under this, he has :

" From the judgment of the Learned and most knowing.

" From the judgment and practice of our Forefathers, and

" From the *plea* and *practice* of such as are against a rule, in their making some use of the rule, and their speaking of right and wrong in singing. It is very natural unto each man, that differs in sentiment from his neighbor, to challenge to himself this honor and happiness, that he is in the right and his neighbor is in the wrong. And it is to be seen in this matter about singing, as well as in any other thing.

" The difference among towns in singing is great. Scarce any two towns that sing perfectly alike, and some differ very much. And yet each town or person asserts they are in the right and their neighbor is in the wrong. Now this is a virtual or implicit yielding and acknowledging that there is some rule, by which a judgment may be made. Upon which I would say only this, Rom. 14, 22. Happy is the man that condemns not himself in the thing he allows. It is an odd thing to blame our neighbors, for going besides, or against rule, whereas, we ourselves acknowledge no rule. But then I would have a remark on these men's making some use of the rule. I have before made mention of this, that our singing was originally owing to rule, and the very rule we plead for ; and that there is some use made of the rule in every song. Wherefore I would reason thus,

If there be no certain rule, why do you make any use of one ? In case there be a rule as your practice declares, why do not you conform wholly to it ? It is beyond the wisest man in the world to reconcile this matter, to wit, How it should be a duty to make some use of the rule, and yet be so heinous a thing to conform wholly to it.

" It is certain men do not usually argue so in other cases. Men can ordinarily see in other things, that the degree does not alter the kind.

" What wise man would judge thus, that it is a lawful thing to read, or to write, but a very abominable thing to read or write exactly and well? Or that it is a lawful thing and a duty to use weights and measures but an intolerable thing to have them exact and true. And yet this is the very case before us. We know assuredly that there is some use made of the rule in common singing. We only plead for an entire conformity to the rule ; and see how it is resented and opposed, as an insufferable thing. And thus I have offered the arguments for the evidence and proof of the assertion laid down. But though there be vastly more evidence and proof, than we have or can have, for many things that we readily own and hold in religion, yet the disaffection of men to the thing and their deep prejudices make light of all the weightiest arguments. And

"Object. 1. This practice leads to the church of England and will bring in organs quickly.

"Ans. 1. In case the thing be a duty we need not be afraid of any ill tendency ; the way of *duty* is the way of *safety*.

"2. It is beyond the wisest man in the world to imagine how skillful singing, should lead or tend to ill, more than unskillful ; we may as well plead that skillful writing or skillfulness in arithmetic tends to ill. There is nothing in the nature of the thing that leads to the church of England.

"3. But suppose it were possible for any to make some ill improvement of it ; it is against the common sense of mankind to reject any ingenious art or science in use among men, because it may be ill improved, or abused by some.

"Because printing is, or may be ill improved unto the venting of the worst errors and heresies, and the most lewd and wicked things that debauch mankind, shall we refuse to use anything that is printed ? Or because a Silversmith could make shrines for Diana, therefore to allow of no such art ?

"4. This argument lies as hard against the common way of singing ; for they pretend to sing the tunes of the church of England.

"5. It is a very strange thing that our forefathers had no sense of this danger and hazard, but that after they were come into this country, they should turn the psalms into new metre, and annex rules to them to sing them by.

" Object. 2. The very original of this way was from the Papists. It came from Rome.

" Ans. 1. I deny not that the Gospel itself came from Rome to England ; we know it did so, and it is very probable that singing came along with the Gospel. I know not of any other coming from Rome but that. And if we must reject Regular Singing on that account, we must by the same reason reject the gospel too. But,

" 2. As for the original of music, *that* was before ever there was a papist, or a church of Rome in the world. It was in great request and flourished much in David's time. David himself was excellently skilled in music, and so were many others in his time. And it is plain it was in use in Moses's time ; and probably known and used before the flood. But,

" 3. Suppose some Papist has written about it, and the papists make use of the art of music in singing, it is very probable it is so, and it is no solid objection against the use of it. There is no reason to reject a thing because a papist has delivered it. If an Angel should preach falsehood we ought to reject it.   And in case a papist or a devil should utter a truth, it is not to be rejected.   It is very true that the papists have horrible errors and corruptions in religion, and that both in Doctrine and practice: yet many of them are learned men, and write well about various arts and sciences, and practice well in some things.   And if we reject everything that the papists hold and do, we must reject a great many things, that are plain duties in religion.   It is enough that we reject what is ill, and as for what is true and good, we should account of it, and embrace it, notwithstanding the papists do hold or practice it.   Phil. 4, 8.   Whatsoever things are true, &c.

   " 4. To take off the force of this objection the guides that we follow in this affair, are ministers or learned men of our own country or persuasion.

   " Object. 3. This way of singing we use in the country is more solemn, and therefore much more suitable and becoming.

   " Ans. 1. If by solemn you mean and intend as the scripture does, there is nothing at all in the plea, for it intends no more but *joyful* and *merry*, and is a word that is almost for ever appropriated to their great feasts, which are attended with the utmost demonstrations of joy, as singing, dancing, instrumental music, &c.

" 2. But suppose by solemn you mean *grave* and *serious*. Nothing makes more against the common way ; for they will readily grant that they use many Quavers and Semiquavers ; &c. And on this very account it is they are pleased with it, and so very loath to part with it. Now all these musical characters belong wholly to airy and vain songs ; neither do we own or allow any of them in the song of the LORD. Judge then which is most solemn.

" Object. 4. It looks very unlikely to be the right way, because that young people fall in with it ; they are not wont to be so forward for anything that is good.

" Ans. 1. As old men are not always wise, so young men are not always fools. Job. 32. 9. Great men, &c.

" 2. Young persons are expressly commanded to praise the LORD. Psalms. 148, 12. Both young men and maidens, &c.

" 3. The same objection was made by the Scribes and Pharisees against Christ's being the true Messiah. The young persons and children owned him, honored him and followed him with their Hosannas, whereas the Scribes, Pharisees and Elderly people rejected him ; and they were very much displeased with the younger people, and would have them rebuked. But the young people were in the right then, and the Elders in the wrong : And so is the case now. The children's learning to praise their great CREATOR and REDEEMER, is very displeasing to some older people. But it is doubtless pleasing to GOD the FATHER and to JESUS CHRIST. Ps. 150. Let everything &c.

" 4. And as for young persons being so forward in the matter, a good account may be given.

" 1. They are generally more free from prejudices, than elderly people. And then besides,

" 2. Their present age disposes them to mirth, and it should be a very joyful and acceptable thing unto elderly people to see them forward to improve their mirth according to scripture directions. Is any merry ? Let him sing Psalms."

Such was the manner in which the " General Association of Connecticut " treated the difficulties under discussion. And we gather from the work, by inference, that the feeling very generally pervaded society affecting it in no common way.

But as storms produce a purer atmosphere and a brighter sky, so these troubles produced a new and more excellent state of things. Schools were soon formed, and well attended, and from their influence, the songs of the Temple were again decently performed. In President Edwards's account of the " Revival of Religion in New England before 1740," published in " The Christian History " [1] for 1743, there is the following record. " Our public praises were then [2] greatly enlivened ; God was then served in our psalmody, in some measure in the *beauty of Holiness*. It has been observable, that there has been scarcely any part of Divine worship, wherein good men amongst us have had grace so drawn forth, and their hearts so lifted up in the ways of God, as in singing his praises. Our congregation excelled all that I ever knew in the external part of the duty before, generally carrying regularly and well, *three parts of music*, and the women a part by themselves. But now they were evidently wont to sing with unusual elevation of heart and voice, which made the duty pleasant indeed."

1735.
During these revivals the complaint was urged — and probably by those who had opposed the cultivation of music — that there was too much singing in religious meetings, and that they used hymns of human composure instead of

---

[1] This was a periodical devoted to the history of revivals, published two years — 1743 and 1744, by Thomas Prince, Jr.

[2] This account relates to the revival of Northampton, in 1734, 1735, and 1736.

the Psalms. How much these complaints affected the interests of religion, or the private comfort of individuals, is not known; but President Edwards deemed them of sufficient importance to devote a chapter of his work on Revivals exclusively to them. There was undoubtedly great joy among the converts, and it did express itself in hymns of praise. But it was indeed strange to complain that they sang God's praise too much. Nor were they contented with objecting to the amount. The time and manner were also denounced. They sang as they went in groups to and from their place of worship; and this was an offence to those who probably had not been satisfied since the musical reformation commenced. To the last objection, President Edwards devoted another chapter; and we refer the reader to his remarks. See " Edwards on Revivals." New York edition, pages 257 and 361.

THE FIRST SINGING-SCHOOLS.

The means of improvement in music, during the reformation, were indeed small. ^{1720.} The number even of tolerable singers could not have been great; and the books for instruction were very few. But the people had espoused the good work of reform, and determined to bear it on.

From the commencement of the Reformation and onward, music grew more and more in favor; and conventions, public lectures, and schools were common. But these were not the first schools in the colonies. There is good reason to believe that schools were known in the early settlement of the country, for Mr. Symmes says in his discourse on the "Reasonableness of Regular Singing:" "The declining from, and getting beside the rule was gradual and insensible. Singing schools and singing books being laid aside, there was no way to learn." See the above-mentioned tract, p. 8; also "Joco Serious Dialogue," p. 4. In this he treats it, as a well-known fact, that schools had previously been in vogue.

Elliot, the Apostle to the Indians was, also, no doubt, in the habit of teaching his converts to sing psalms, while he taught them the first principles of Christianity. Their singing was spoken of by Dr. Mather, as being "most ravishing." It is certain he paid so much attention to their psalmody, that he had translated the psalms into Indian verse, and published them, before he completed more of the Bible than the New Testament; and giving them psalms, can we believe he would neglect the music?

1720. In 1720, we find singing societies formed in different parts of New England, for promoting Regular Singing; and before these, as lectures, were delivered some of the best essays upon music that have been preserved. From these societies, singing-schools, so long neglected, were revived; and probably the societies themselves were in part singing-schools, or rather singing meetings.[1] It is certain that they had for one part of their design, at least, *the collecting and diffusing of musical knowledge.* Hence musical subjects were discussed before them. Another part of their design undoubtedly was, *to cultivate and improve the style of their Church Music.* These societies or schools appear to have been the first extensively organized effort for that purpose in this country. They were to them schools, although not conducted exactly as schools are at this day. However little of elementary instruction there might have been at first, they were the germs of

[1] " We are in possession of an anecdote, which seems to fix the era when singing by note was first introduced into the churches at Boston. Mr. Timothy Burbank, who died in Plymouth, Oct. 13th, 1793, aged 90, was born at Malden, and during his apprenticeship at the tailor's trade, in Boston, attended Dr. Colman's meeting. He was always uniform in relating that he attended the first singing school, and religious society which introduced singing by notes, at Boston. This era, therefore, must have been between the years 1717 and 1724. Mr. B. was a chorister many years at Plymouth, also an officer in the militia." See Mass. Hist. Col. second series, vol. 4, p. 30.

those schools, for which New England has ever
since been remarkable.

The most influential of the clergy, encouraged
the cultivation of music; and the study of it was,
during the controversy, revived in the college.
Mr. Symmes says in his Dialogue, p. 14 : " It
was known and approved of in our College from
the very foundation of it ; and though for some
years of later time it was unhappily neglected, yet,
blessed be God, it is again revived, and I hope it
may ever be continued in that school of the
Prophets."

WHERE THE REFORM BEGAN.

While the clergy, as they ever ought, were
urging on the work of reform in the music of their
churches, the people were fast coming over to their
faith, and earnestly laboring to carry out their
schemes. The first churches to reform and improve their music, were those in Boston, Roxbury,
Dorchester, Cambridge, Taunton, Bridgewater,
Charlestown, Ipswich, Newbury, Andover and
Bradford. See Cases of Conscience, published in
1723, page 7.

CLERICAL INFLUENCE.

The Reformation was a noble triumph of good

men in a good cause. But it was not done without labor. The clergy prepared, and preached upon the duty of improving their church music, with the same directness and pungency, as upon other subjects of Christian duty. Nor did they deem that in speaking *once* they had done their *whole duty,* and perhaps laid in a store of good works to balance some former delinquency. One of the most venerable of their number, had three discourses printed, in three successive years, that were prepared for, and preached to his own people, as well as to neighboring congregations. Nor did they rely exclusively upon their own preaching; but every man called in his neighbor's aid; so that each one by exchanging, preached his sermon upon music many times; and each congregation had the privilege of hearing their duty set forth by different men.

There was great ability in the discussion, but there was still greater zeal. Not only did they preach to their own, and as they had opportunity to neighboring congregations, but they also preached from house to house, " in season and out of season." Associations of the clergy met to deliberate upon this neglected subject; and to them were submitted, and by them sanctioned, several of the tracts that were circulated among the people.   How widely these tracts were circulated cannot now be told ; or how many more there were published that the desolating hand of time has not permitted to reach us. It is wonderful if one half of the tracts then printed has been preserved.   And if so many were printed for circulation, what must that number be, that was preached, but never met the public eye ! In our research on this subject, we have been able to find *ten* lengthy tracts — each equivalent to a long sermon. Three of these were written by the Rev. Dr. Symmes ; two by Dr. Cotton Mather ; one by the Rev. Mr. Dwight ; one by the Rev. Thomas Walter ; one by the Rev. Mr. Chauncey, of Durham, Ct., and the others, each indorsed by several ministers.

MUSIC HELD SACRED.

The church music of our forefathers before the Reformation in 1720, was held as most sacred. The tunes were supposed to be holy ; "and that as much reverence should be shown to them, as to the psalms themselves."   It was the custom of the people, " to put off their hats, and put on a great show of devotion and gravity, whenever psalm-tunes were sung, though there were not one word of a psalm."   See " Reasonableness of Regular Singing," p. 18.

MUSIC IN USE.

The music before the public at this time was Ravenscroft's book which had been used in the colonies since their first settlement ; Playford's collection, which was published in England, in 1671 ; that added to their psalm-books ; the small works by Mr. Tufts; and Mr. Walter's Singing Book. The two English books were possessed by very few individuals ; and the music in the psalm-book was most general among the people. The compositions, being those of the English masters, were of a high character. The music was of the old choral style, the church's only style of free melody. From the time Mr. Walter published his singing-book, on-ward, it was the favorite, and there was a constant demand for the work, to supply the schools and singing societies, so that it passed through several editions in a very few years.

WALTER'S INTRODUCTION.

The people did not believe that music could be learned so as to sing a *new* tune without first hear-ing it. The same impression, might but a short time since, and perhaps may even now, be found, existing in the interior of Pennsylvania. But that must be a lamentable degree of ignorance on the subject, which could ever suggest such a belief.

On this subject, Mr. Walter says, in the Introduction to his Singing-book, " Singing is reducible to the *rules of art* ; and he who makes himself Master of a few of these rules is able at *first sight* to sing hundreds of new tunes, which he never saw or heard before, and this by the bare inspection of the notes, without hearing them from the mouth of a singer. Just as a person who has learnt all the rules of reading is able to read any new book, without any further help or instruction. This is a truth, although known to, and proved by many of us, yet very hardly to be received, and credited in the country." . . . .

1721.

The following extract from the same introduction will further illustrate the sentiments entertained by both parties. " These rules then will be serviceable upon a *threefold* account. First. They will instruct us in the right and true singing of the tunes that are already in use in our churches, which, when they first came out of the hands of the composers of them, were sung according to the rules of *the scale of music*, but are now miserably tortured, and twisted, and quavered, in some churches, into a horrid medley of confused and disorderly noises. This must necessarily create a most disagreeable jar in the ears of all that can judge better of singing than these men, who please themselves with their own ill-sounding *echoes*. For to compare small things with great, our Psalmody has suffered the like inconveniences which our Faith had labored under, in case it had been committed, and trusted to the uncertain and doubtful conveyance of *Oral Tradition*. Our tunes are, for want of a standard to appeal to in all our singing, left to the mercy of every unskilful throat, to chop and alter, twist and change, according to their infinitely divers, and no less odd humours and fancies. That this is most true, I appeal to the experience of those who have happened to be present in many of our congregations, who will grant me, that there are no two churches that sing alike. Yea I have myself heard, for instance, *Oxford tune* sung in *three* churches, (which I purposely forbear to mention) with as much difference as there can possibly be between *York* and *Oxford*, or any two other different tunes. Therefore any man that pleads with me for what they call the *Old Way*, I can confute him only by making this demand, ' *What is the Old Way*,' Which I am sure they cannot tell. For one town says, theirs is the true *old way*, another town thinks the same of theirs, and so does a third of their way of tuning it. But let such men know, that the writer of this pamphlet, (who can sing all the various twistings of the old way, and that too, according to the *genius* of most congregations, as well as they can any one way ; which must therefore make him a better judge than they are or can be ;) affirms, that the notes sung according to the *Scale and Rules of Music,* are the *true Old Way.* For somebody or other did compose our tunes, and did they, think ye, compose them by *rule* or by *rote ?* If the latter, how came they pricked down in our Psalm Books ? And this I am sure of, we sing them, as they are there pricked down, and I am sure the country people do not. Judge ye then, who is in the right. Nay I am sure if you would once be at the pains to learn our way of singing, you could not but be convinced of what I now affirm. But our tunes have passed through strange *Metamorphoses* (beyond those of Ovid) since their first introduction into the world. But to return to the standard from which we have so long departed cannot fail to set all to rights, and to reduce our sacred songs to their primitive form and composition.

" Again it will serve for the introduction of more tunes into the divine service ; and these, tunes of no small pleasancy and variety, which

will in a great measure render this part of worship
still more delightful to us. For at present we are
confined to *eight* or *ten* tunes, and in some congregations to little more than half that number,
which being so often sung over, are too apt, if not
to create a distaste, yet at least, mightily to lessen
the relish of them.

" There is one more advantage which will
accrue from the instructions of this little book;
and that is this, That by the just and equal *timing*
of the notes, our singing will be reduced to an
exact length, so as not to fatigue the singer with a
tedious protraction of the notes beyond the compass of a man's breath, and the power of his
spirit; — a fault very frequent in the country,
where I myself have twice in one note paused to
take breath. The *keeping of time* in singing will
have this natural effect upon us that the whole
assembly shall begin and end every single note, and
every line exactly together, to an instant, which is
a wonderful beauty in singing, when a great number of voices are together sounding forth the divine praises. But for want of this, I have observed
in many places, one man is upon this note, while
another is a note before him, which produces
something so hideous and disorderly as is beyond
expression bad. And then the even, unaffected,

and smooth sounding the notes, and the omission of those unnatural Quaverings and turnings will serve to prevent all that discord and lengthy tediousness which is so often a fault in our singing of psalms.   For much time is taken up in shaking out these *turns* and *quavers*; and beside no two men in the congregation quaver alike, or together; which sounds in the ears of a good judge, like *five hundred* different tunes roared out at the same time, whose perpetual interferings with one another, perplexed jars, and unmeasured periods, would make a man wonder at the false pleasure which they conceive in that which good judges of music and sounds, cannot bear to hear."

MR. SECOMB'S SERMON.

After the discussions had ceased, and the virulence of feeling had passed away, there was in the minds of the people a fixed determination to pursue the good work which was as yet only begun. The arguments had not been lost.   They had been treasured in the mind ; the people saw their duty and determined to do it.

In the year 1741, we find, the feeling
1741. still alive, and an advocate still before the people, in the person of the Rev. Mr. Secomb. We shall make but a very brief extract, to show

his ideas in reference to the duty of cultivating music.

" If God has given us strong Lungs and tunable Voices they should be used in Singing. Mere mental Music is too refined, for those who have Senses so quick and strong: and those curious Organs, which God has made so fit for this Purpose, so helpful in such Exercises, these are evidently designed by our Creator, to be used for his Glory. It is a great Beauty and Ornament to this heavenly Duty to be regular and uniform in it: Therefore we should make Conscience of learning the several Tunes which render this most angelic Exercise, harmonious and pleasant. A variety is tasteful and suitable to the Nature of Man, to the Affections and Passions, Virtues and Graces which are moved by the Various Occurrences which he meets with. The greater variety we have of Tunes, sung in a serious and regular, sweet and Solemn Manner, the more is the devout Soul raised in rapturous Joy or melted into ingenuous Grief, or otherwise moved agreeably to the Matter of the Psalm.

" How delightfully did the heavenly Host sing at the Birth of the Saviour ? How often are we entertained with the elevating Songs of the Heavenly Choirs in the Revelation ? These reprove our bad

Ears, our unmusical Souls ; we are check'd as the
pious Mr. Baily tho't himself ; when he refused to
sing with his dying Consort, the Angels sang
Melodiously."

FIRST AMERICAN ORGAN.

1745.   The first organ built in this country was
made by Edward Bromfield, Jr. of Boston.
The following description of it, written by the
Rev. Thomas Prince, minister of the Old South
Church, in Boston, is copied from the Panoplist,
vol. ii. p. 194.   Speaking of Mr. Bromfield's
accomplishments he says:

" As he was well skilled in Music, he for exercise and recreation, with his own hands, has made
a most accurate Organ, with two rows of keys and
many hundred pipes ; his intention being twelve
hundred, but died before he completed it.   The
workmanship of the keys and pipes, surprisingly
nice and curious, exceeding any thing of the kind
that ever came here from England ; which he designed not merely to refresh his spirits but with
harmony to mix, enliven and regulate his vocal and
delightful songs to his great Creator, Preserver,
Benefactor, and Redeemer.   He thought the
Author of Nature and Music, does, by his early

chorusters of the Air, with which the day spring rises, teach us to awake with them, and begin our morning exercise with grateful hymns of joy and praises to him. And what is surprising was, that he had but a few times looked into the inside work of two or three organs which came from England."

" Mr. Bromfield was born at Boston in 1723 — entered Harvard College in 1738 — took his first degree in 1742 — his second in 1745, and died at his father's house, August 18, 1746, to the deep regret of all who knew him."

" From his childhood he was thoughtful, calm, easy, modest, of tender affections, dutiful to his superiors, and kind to all about him. As he grew up these agreeable qualities ripened in him ; and he appeared very ingenious, observant, curious, penetrating, especially in works of nature, in mechanical contrivances and manual operations, which increased upon his studying the mathematical sciences, as also in searching into the truths of divine revelation, and into the nature of genuine experimental piety."

HISTORY OF BOOKS,

CHRONOLOGICALLY ARRANGED.

WATTS'S PSALMS.

1741. In 1741, Dr. Franklin published at Philadelphia, an edition of Dr. Watts's Hymns; and the same year an edition of the Psalms was published at Boston, for J. Edwards. These we believe were the first editions of that work published in this country. The Psalms and Hymns were bound separately, well printed on good paper, and altogether making two small, but very neat volumes.

Where or when they were first used in the colonies, the writer knows not. Doubtless some congregations were supplied with English books before an edition was published in this country; for the design was favorably known in the colonies, even before they were published in England.

While yet the author, Dr. Watts, had completed only a few specimens of his work, he sent them in a manuscript, written by his own hand, to Dr. Cotton Mather, of Boston, asking his opinion of the poems,[1] as a specimen of a work he intended to write and publish. Dr. Mather complimented both the design and the execution ; and whether his opinion had any influence or not, Dr. Watts went on with the work publishing in parts, from time to

[1] The following is a copy of Dr. Watts's letter accompanying the manuscript.

"To my honored and dear friend, Dr. Cotton Mather of New England.

" Rev. and Dear Sir,

" I may persuade myself of a hearty acceptance of this little present I make you. They are the fruits of some easy hours this last year, wherein I have not sought poetical flourish, but simplicity of style and verse for the use of vulgar christians.

" 'Tis not a translation of David that I pretend ; but an imitation of him so nearly in christian hymns that the Jewish Psalmist may plainly appear, yet leave Judaism behind. My little Essay that attends this manuscript, will render some of my reasons for this way of introducing the ancient Psalms in the worship of the N. T.

" The notes I have frequently inserted at the end, are chiefly to render the world a reason for the particular liberties I assumed in each Psalm.

" If I may be so happy as to have your free censure and judgment of 'em it will help me in correcting others by them. I entreat you Sir, that none of them may steal out into public. If God allow me one year more, even under my present weaknesses, I hope he will enable me to finish my design. To him be all the Glory. Amen. Your most affectionate Lover, and obliged friend.   I. WATTS.

" London March 17th,

"1717 – 18."

time, as he wrote, until in the spring of 1719, he completed the whole. Probably it was not used in the colonial churches at all, till after the Reformation of 1720, and perhaps not till near the time of their publication as above. But whether it was in a few instances or not, Watts was not substituted for the Bay Psalm Book generally, until after the American Revolution. Then the change became the subject of warm and spirited discussions. The people were divided ; some were determined to make the change at all hazards, while others deemed it a most sacrilegious act.

TATE AND BRADY'S PSALMS.

1741.   Not far from this time — 1741 — there was an edition of Tate and Brady's [1] " book of Psalms in Metre," published in the colonies. This was used in a few churches before Watts was introduced ; but how extensively it was used, or at what time it was published, the writer has no means of knowing.

It is from this work, that the psalms used in the

---

[1] Tate and Brady were two English poets. Nahum Tate was born at Dublin, in 1652, and was poet laureate to William III. He died in 1715. Nicholas Brady, D. D. was an English Episcopalian divine, born in 1659, and died in 1726. They published their work before 1696, for " this version was licensed " during that year, " and was used in most of the churches in England and Ireland."

"Protestant Episcopal Church, in the United States of America," were taken. They are selections from this, throwing aside a very considerable portion of the whole work. And when the committee made the selections, they also took the liberty — as others have too freely done — to make such alterations as seemed to them desirable.

BARNARD'S PSALMS.

In 1752, another attempt to improve our metrical psalmody, was made by the Rev. 1752. Mr. Barnard. He turned the psalms into verse, and composed a few hymns, which were published at Boston. This book was entitled, " A new version of the Psalms of David ; fitted to the tunes used in the churches ; With several Hymns out of the Old and New Testament. By John Barnard, Pastor of a church in Marblehead."

In his Preface, he says : " Though the New England version of the Psalms of David, in Metre, is generally very good, and few of the same age may be compared with it, yet the flux of Languages has rendered several phrases in it obsolete, and the mode of expression in various places less acceptable ; for which reason an amendment or new version has been long, and greatly, desired by the most judicious among us.

" After waiting long for the performance of some more masterly pen, and upon repeated desires, I have ventured to employ all the spare time of near upon the last three years of my advanced age, (this day through the forbearance of God completing my seventieth year,) in composing a new version, suited to the tunes used in our churches, which by Divine assistance is now finished."

At the end of this book, were sixteen pages of handsomely engraved music, with bars ; in all containing fifty different tunes. These are of the choral style; such as London, Windsor, Mear, &c. At the end of the book were printed forty-eight tunes, in three parts, well engraved, with bars ; and immediately before the music is one page of elementary instruction.

Mr. Allen and Mr. Elliot agree in their biographical sketches, in limiting the use of Mr. Barnard's work to his own congregation.

BAY PSALMS REVISED.

In 1758, Rev. Thomas Prince; A. M. revised " the Bay Psalm Book," and it was published with the following title : " The . Psalms, Hymns and Spiritual Songs of the Old and New Testament faithfully translated into English Metre. Being the New England Psalm-Book revised and

improved by an endeavour after a yet nearer ap-
proach to the Inspired Original, as well as to the
rules of Poetry. With an addition of fifty other
Hymns on the most important subjects of Christianity, with their titles placed in order, from the Fall
of Angels and Men, to Heaven after the General
Judgment."

These revised psalms and hymns were doubtless
used in some of the churches, if not in most, but
to what extent is not certainly known. The
work had been almost the only one in use from its
first publication, and continued to be in some
churches until superseded by Watts. A second
edition was published in 1773.

URANIA.

In 1761, a book of music was published with
the following title. "URANIA. Or a choice collection of Psalm Tunes, Anthems, and Hymns,
from the most approved authors, with some entirely new: In *two, three,* and *four* parts: The
whole peculiarly adapted to the use of churches
and private families. To which are prefaced the
plainest and most necessary Rules of Psalmody.
By James Lyons, A. B. Philadelphia. Price 15s."

This book was much larger than any previous
work that had been published in the colonies.

Report says that it ruined the publisher. It was handsomely engraved by Henry Dawkins; and printed on excellent English paper. It contained twelve pages of elementary instruction, and about two hundred pages of music; ninety of which were occupied with anthems. The arrangement of the harmony was bad, showing the editor to have been but little acquainted with musical science. In many places the harmony could scarcely have been worse. Dissonant chords are seldom used. In a few cases, the chord of the added sixth may be found at a cadence; and in a few more, the strange idea of a seventh taken at the cadence on the subdominant; but in no one instance is one found on the dominant. This work contained the first music of a fuguing style ever published in this country. Not quite one half of the psalm-tunes were of the plain choral style, and the rest were of a light or fuguing character. The anthems were characterized by poor attempts at fugue and imitation with long runs in the melody.

The following was his dedication.

" To the Clergy of every Denomination in America.

" Reverend Sirs,

" Relying on the evident propriety of your patronising this Publication, permit me to lay Urania at your feet.

" Should the following Collection of tunes be so fortunate as to merit your Approbation : To please the taste of the Public : To assist the private Christian in his dayly devotion : And to improve in any degree, an important part of Divine Service in the Colonies, for which it was designed, I shall think myself happy in being the Editor, notwithstanding the great expense, labor and anxiety it has cost me to complete it.

" May you long continue ornaments of your profession ; Dayly see abundant fruits of your labor in the Reformation of mankind ; And incessantly enjoy those sublime Pleasures which nothing but a series of rational and virtuous actions, can create.

" I am, Reverend Gentlemen,

Your most obedient,

And humble servant,

JAMES LYON."

FLAGG'S BOOK.

In 1764, a new collection of church music was compiled and published by Mr. Josiah Flagg, of Boston. It was entitled : " A collection of the best Psalm Tunes, in two, three, and four parts ; from the most approved authors, fitted to all measures, and approved of by the best masters in

Boston, New England ; to which are added some Hymns and Anthems ; the greater part of them never before printed in America. By Josiah Flagg. Engraved by Paul Revere ; Printed and sold by him and Josiah Flagg, Boston, 1764."

This was the largest work, except Lyon's, yet published in this country. It had *one hundred and sixteen tunes, and two anthems.* The style of the music was much lighter than any previous work ; containing every variety, from Old Hundred, to the " March of Richard, Third." The harmony was generally poor. The dominant seventh and its inversions were not used, except in two or three tunes, selected from Battishill and Riley. Modulations sometimes occur in one part, without the corresponding motion in the others ; with many other irregularities. The tunes are generally written in four parts, and the principal melody given to the tenors. This is the first American book in which the music was written in four parts. Selections are made from Tansur, Dr. Worgan, Battishill and others. There were also some American compositions ; but, the names not being given, the authors, and number of tunes, are unknown. That there were some, is plainly inferred from the preface, in which he says : " We are obliged to the other side the Atlantic chiefly,

for our tunes." The work contained only three
pages of elementary instruction; of which, he
says : " The Rules laid down, though concise, are
plain, and contain the whole that is necessary."

Although but one other new book had been
published in the colonies since Mr. Walter's, and
very few English works had been circulated, the
author felt called upon to apologize for offering to
the public a new collection; and he says in his
preface; " It may possibly be thought necessary,
that some apology should be made, for offering to
the public, a new collection of Psalm-tunes, at a
time when there are already so many among us.
The Editor has only this to say in general, that he
has endeavoured, according to the best of his judgment, to extract the sweets out of a variety of fra-
grant flowers. He has taken from every author he
has seen, a few tunes, which he judges to be the
best, and comprized them within the compass of a
small pocket volume ; [1] how far he has succeeded
in this attempt, he leaves to the candid masters of
Music to determine. If he is so fortunate as to
meet with their approbation, with regard to the
choice he has made, he begs leave, upon the sup-

---

[1] This work was the same size as most singing books are at this
day. Then, every book was called a "pocket volume," that was not
a folio or a quarto.

position, just to make this remark; that as the tunes were composed by different masterly hands, the Air of them is various, which affords reason to hope they will not fail of gratifying in some measure persons of every taste."

This work was very well engraved in *round notes*, and was the first book of music printed on paper manufactured in the colonies. He says of this: "It is hoped, it will not diminish the value of this book in the estimation of any, but may in some degree recommend it, even to those who have no peculiar relish for the music, that however we are obliged to the other side the Atlantic chiefly, for our tunes, the paper on which they are printed, is the manufacture of our own country."

BAYLEY'S BOOK.

In the same year as the above, 1764, Mr. Bayley, of Newburyport, Mass. published a small work, entitled: "A new and complete introduction to the Grounds and Rules of Music, in two books.

BOOK I.

"Containing the Grounds and Rules of Music; or an introduction to the art of singing by note, taken from Thomas Walter, A. M.

BOOK II.

" Containing a new and correct introduction to the
Grounds of Music, rudimental and practical ; from
William Tansur's Royal Melody ; the whole being
a collection of a variety of the choicest tunes from
the most approved Masters.

" O, praise ye the Lord, prepare your glad voice, his
praise in the great assembly to sing.   Ps. 149, 1.

" Printed for and sold by, Bulkly Emerson, and
Daniel Bayley of Newburyport, 1764."

This work contained thirty-four tunes.   They
were neatly engraved by John W. Gilman, of Exe-
ter, in a diamond shaped note.   The style of the
music is nearly that of Mr. Walter's, or the choral
style.   The only three tunes at all removed from
it, are St. Luke's, St Martin's, and Weston Flavel.
The others are like St. David's, Windsor, York,
&c.   The tunes are all arranged in *three* parts,
base, treble and tenor.   Some are copied literally
from Mr. Walter ; while one, at least, bears the
mark in the style, as well as the name, of an
American composition.   But of this we are not
certain, as the author's names are in no instance
given.

Three editions of this work were published in
the same year, 1764.   Two were printed at New-

buryport; one for Bulkley Emerson, containing thirty-four tunes; and the other for the author, Mr. Bayley, containing fourteen additional tunes. The third was printed at Salem, Mass. for Mascholl Williams. These were all printed from the same plates; but the title pages and introductions were typographical, and from different forms.

THE NEW ENGLAND PSALM SINGER.

In 1770, Mr. Billings published his first work. It was entitled: " The New England Psalm-Singer: or American Chorister. Containing a number of Psalm-tunes, Anthems and Canons. In Four and Five Parts. (Never before published.) Composed by William Billings, a Native of Boston, in New England. Math. 21, 16. Out of the Mouth of Babes and Sucklings hast thou perfected Praise. James 5, 13. Is any Merry? Let him sing Psalms.

> O, praise the Lord with one consent,
>   And in this grand design,
> Let Britain and the Colonies
>   Unanimously join.

Boston: New England. Printed by Edes & Gill."

This opened a new era for the history of psalmody in the colonies. The churches were at that time passing another mutation in the matter of their music. Watts's Psalms and Hymns were then just being substituted for the Bay Psalm Book and other works. Billings saw the desire for change, and threw into the current of feeling, a style of music differing from that in use, but yet not so widely, as to violate their prejudices. This for him was the time for success; the tide of affairs all moved in his favor. The cultivation of music had been increasing since the time of the Reformation, in 1720; and the increased demand for music, was, as yet, but imperfectly supplied. The works that had preceded his, had afforded but a small variety; his gave more; and as the last and greatest charm, it was the first American composition ever published in this country; and bearing a spice of patriotism on its pages, it became in that patriotic day, except with the critics, quite popular.

The New England Psalm-Singer contained twenty-two pages of elementary instruction; and, prefixed, a preface and an " Essay on the nature and properties of musical sound," that occupied ten pages. The Essay was written either by Dr. Charles Stockbridge, of Scituate, Mass. or the Rev. Dr. Byles. In the body of the work, there were one hundred and eight pages, containing

about one hundred and twenty tunes, together
with several anthems. The tunes possessed considerable variety in character, and more variety
in metre, than any previous work. In the harmony, he took all the liberties one could desire,
either with or without knowledge. To illustrate
his views on the subject of harmony, we make a
few extracts from his remarks upon composition,
offered, "To all Musical Practitioners:" "Perhaps it may be expected by some, that I should
say something concerning Rules for Composition;
to these I answer that *Nature is the best Dictator*,
for all the hard dry studied Rules that ever were
prescribed, will not enable any person to form an
Air, any more than the bare Knowledge of the
four and twenty letters, and strict Grammatical
Rules will qualify a Scholar for composing a piece
of Poetry, or properly adjusting a Tragedy without
a Genius. It must be Nature, Nature must lay
the foundation, Nature must inspire the Thought.
. . . . For my own part, as I dont think
myself confined to any Rules for Composition laid
down by any that went before me, neither should
I think (were I to pretend to lay down rules) that
any who come after me were any ways obligated
to adhere to them, any further than they should
think proper: So in fact I think it is best for every

Composer to be his own Carver. Therefore, upon this consideration, for me to dictate, or pretend to prescribe Rules of this Nature for others, would not only be very unnecessary but also a very great piece of Vanity."

In style, the "New England Psalm-Singer" differed but little from that of "Williams's Collection," an English work, that was republished four years after, by Mr. Bayley. But it differed materially from the music in general use; and yet more from the numerous books that immediately followed it. These are so numerous, that we cannot mention them particularly, yet must give an imperfect list [1] of such as we have seen, to show the increased demand for books, as an evidence of the increase of musical cultivation. We have arranged them in the order of time, as they were published.

[1] This list is made from our own and from Mr. Mason's large collection of old American books; and we are sorry that we have it not in our power to give it entire down to the year 1800. With a little attention the friends of music could easily complete the list, which should be deposited in the Massachusetts Historical Library, as a relic of the past worth preserving, not so much for their intrinsic value, as for their historical character. In the future, they would tell the history of the past, far more impressively than the page of history.

11

LIST OF WORKS PUBLISHED BEFORE 1800.

1774.
"THE AMERICAN HARMONY: *or Royal Melody Complete.* ' In two volumes.' Vol. 1. By William Tansur. Printed and sold by Daniel Bayley, Newbury Port, 1774. Vol. II. The American Harmony ; or Universal Psalmodist. By A. Williams, Teacher of Psalmody in London. Printed and sold by Daniel Bayley, Newbury Port. Jan. 13, 1774." Each volume contained 96 pages.

1774.
"THE GENTLEMAN AND LADIES MUSICAL COMPANION ; — containing a variety of excellent Anthems, Psalm tunes, &c. collected from the best Authors ; with a short explanation of the rules of music. The whole corrected and rendered plain. By John Stickney. 1774. Printed and sold by Daniel Bayley, Newbury Port, and by most booksellers in New England."

1778.
"THE SINGING-MASTER'S ASSISTANT : or Key to Practical Music : Being an abridgment from ' The New England Psalm-Singer,' together with several other tunes never before published. Boston. Draper and Folsom. Engraved by Benjamin Pierpont. June, 1778." 104 pages.

"THE NORTHAMPTON COLLECTION, By Elias Mann. Nov. 3, 1778."

" MUSIC IN MINIATURE, Containing a col- 1779. lection of Psalm tunes of various metres, set in score. Engraved by B. Johnson. Printed and sold by the Author. (William Billings.) Boston, 1779. 32 pp. This work was designed to be bound up with their Psalm Books, and was principally selected from different Authors."

" A COLLECTION of the best and most ap- 1779. proved Tunes and Anthems, for the promotion of Psalmody. By Andrew Law. 1779."

" THE PSALM-SINGERS AMUSMENT: Con- 1781. taining a number of Fuguing pieces and Anthems. Composed by WILLIAM BILLINGS, author of the Singing Master's Assistant. Printed and sold by the Author, at his house near the White Horse. Boston. 1781." J. Norman, Sculptor. 104 pages.

" A COLLECTION OF HYMNS AND TUNES, 1782. printed at Cheshire, Ct. By Andrew Law, 1782."

" RUDIMENTS OF MUSIC, by A. LAW. 1783. 1783."

" SELECT HARMONY, Containing the Neces- 1783. sary rules of Psalmody, together with a Collection of approved Psalm tunes, Hymns and Anthems. By Oliver Brownson." I. Sanford, Sculp. 1783.

1784.   " THE MASSACHUSETTS HARMONY ; being a new collection of Psalm tunes, Fugues and Anthems, selected from the most approved Authors, ancient and modern.   By a Lover of Harmony.   Boston.   Printed for, and sold by, John Norman, at his shop in Marshall Lane."

This work was published subsequent to Billings's Singing Master's Assistant, for it extracts from that ; but the year is not mentioned either in the title page or in the preface.   The style of the music was that of the day ;   inelegant melody and worse harmony, filled with the most miserable attempts at fugue.   The seventh and its inversions were wholly avoided.   The compiler says :   " I must confess, I dont think it absolutely necessary to introduce discords into the composition of a tune, in order to have some discovered in performing it." On the cover, in gilt, was the name of " Samuel Boardman, Jun., Lynn, 1784 ; " so it must have been published between the years 1778 and 1784.

1785.   " INTRODUCTORY LESSONS, practiced by the Uranian Society, held at Philadelphia, for promoting the knowledge of Vocal Music. Jan. 1, 1785."

1786.   " THE SUFFOLK HARMONY.   Consisting of Psalm tunes, Fugues, and Anthems.   By William Billings.   Engraved and printed by J. Norman for the author.   Boston, 1786.   56 pp."

" SELECT HARMONY. An original work, by A. Law. Baltimore. Jan. 7, 1786." 1786.

" LAUS DEO! The Worcester Collection of Sacred Harmony. The whole compiled for the use of Schools and Singing Societies, and recommended by many approved Teachers of Psalmody. Printed Typographically, at Worcester, Mass. By Isaiah Thomas," Jan. 1786. Pages 198. 1786.

This is an interesting work, from the fact of its being the first book *printed typographically* in this country. All previous works had been engraved. We extract the following information from the preface.

" Having observed with pleasure the attention paid to church music, by most classes of people in the N. E. States, and knowing many of the books now in use, necessarily high-charged, owing to their being printed from copper-plates, he " (the Publisher) " was induced both by inclination, and at the request of several friends, to attempt a work of this kind from types; hoping to afford it somewhat cheaper, than any other book of its bigness printed after the usual manner. He accordingly engaged a set of musical types to be made in England for this purpose by one of the most ingenious Type Founders in Great Britain, which he hopes, on inspection of the tunes, will be found to have answered the purpose." [1]

The typography is good ; a fair round note, and well distributed.

In 1788, " The Second Edition with large additions," was printed *Typographically* at Worcester.

In 1797, " The Sixth Edition, altered, corrected, and revised, with additions by Oliver Holden," was printed *Typographically*, at Boston, by Isaiah Thomas and Ebenezer T. Andrews.

From the preface of the sixth edition, we extract the following. " The subscriber " (Isaiah Thomas) " informs his musical friends who have so liberally encouraged the five former editions of the Worcester Collection, that he has contracted with Mr. Oliver Holden, who is interested in the work, to compile and correct the present and future editions, which he presumes will be pleasing to its patrons."

Mr. Holden edited three editions.

1788.   " THE CHORISTER's COMPANION : containing besides the necessary rules of Psalmody, a

---

[1] From this little sketch we are induced to believe, that this work is the first printed by type in this country, and perhaps the first musical typography known. Mr. Thomas, however, in his History of Printing, has not spoken of the subject at all ; and the writer has no means of knowing, whether musical type was known in Europe or not, before that time.

choice and valuable collection of Psalm-tunes, Hymns and Anthems, from the most celebrated ancient and modern authors; together with several tunes never before published. By Simeon Jocelin, New Haven, 1788."

" FEDERAL HARMONY: in three parts. Part I. An Introduction to the Art of Singing. Part II. A large collection of Psalm Tunes. Part III. Select Anthems, &c. Boston, Nov. 11, 1788." 1788.

" DIVINE SONGS " — " In three and four parts. By Abraham Wood. Northborough, March, 1789." Pages 32. 1789.

" HARMONIA AMERICANA. Containing a concise introduction to the grounds of Music, with a variety of Airs suitable for Divine Worship, and the use of Musical Societies, consisting of three and four parts. By Samuel Holyoke, A. B. Boston, Jan. 24, 1791."

" AMERICAN HARMONY. ' In three and four parts. The whole entirely new.' By Oliver Holden, Teacher of Music in Charlestown, Sept. 27, 1792." Pages 32.

" MUSICAL MAGAZINE, No. 1. By Andrew Law. 1792." This work was a yearly periodical.

" SUPPLEMENT TO THE CHORISTER'S COMPANION, Containing 16 pages of Psalm and Hymn tunes, newly composed, or not before printed in America. By Simeon Jocelin.   New Haven, Feb. 1, 1792."

" THE RURAL HARMONY, being an original composition, in three and four parts ; for the use of singing schools and Musical Societies.   By Jacob Kimball, Jun. A. B. Boston, 1793." Printed typographically.

" THE UNION HARMONY, or Universal Collection of Sacred Music. In two volumes. By Oliver Holden, Author of the American Harmony. Boston, 1793."

" COLUMBIAN HARMONY, by Joseph Stone and Abraham Wood.   Boston, Sept. 13, 1793."

" SACRED LINES for Thanksgiving Day, Nov. 9, 1793.   Written and set to Music by Hans Gram, Organist to Brattle Street Church, Boston.   To which is set several Psalm tunes by the same composer.   Boston, 1793."

" COLUMBIAN HARMONY, No. 1. By Daniel Read. 1793."   (See Mr. Read's Biography.)

" MUSICAL MAGAZINE, No. 2.   By A. Law. June 19, 1793."

" THE PSALMODIST'S COMPANION."   A compilation.   By Jacob French, Author of the New American Melody.   Boston, 1793.

" MASSACHUSETTS COMPILER, by Holden, Gram, and Holyoke.   Boston, 1794."   (See their biographies.)

"THE CONTINENTAL HARMONY," Composed by William Billings. Boston, 1794. Pages 199.

"THE ART OF SINGING; in three parts. Part I. The Musical Primer. Part II. The Christian Harmony. Part III. The Musical Magazine. Baltimore, April 8, 1794."

"THE MUSICAL MAGAZINE, No. 3. Baltimore, Oct. 9, 1794."

"THE HARMONY OF MAINE," being an original composition of Psalm and Hymn tunes. By S. Belcher, of Farmington, Lincoln Co. Me. 1794.

"THE RESPONSARY: containing a collection of church music, set with second trebles instead of counters. By Amos Bull, of Hartford, Ct. 1795."

"MUSICAL MAGAZINE, No. 4. Baltimore, April 4, 1795."

"THE MIDDLESEX HARMONY: being an original composition, in three and four parts. By Samuel Babcock, Watertown, Dec. 1795."

"THE VOCAL INSTRUCTOR. By Benjamin Dearborn. Feb. 28, 1796."

"THE COLUMBIAN REPOSITORY. By Samuel Holyoke." The date of this is not known. (See biography.)

"THE HARMONIST'S COMPANION. Composed by Daniel Belknap, teacher of music in Framingham. Sept. 11, 1797."

" THE UNITED STATES SACRED HARMONY. A compilation, by Amos Pilsbury. Charleston, S. C. July, 1799." This work had quite an extensive circulation.

" HARMONIA CŒLESTIS. A collection of church music in two, three and four parts ; with words adapted to each ; comprehending not only the metres in common use, but the particular metres in the Hartford Collection of Hymns ; the tunes correctly figured for the Organ and Harpsichord, with an introduction to music. Chiefly collected from the greatest masters in Europe ; and never before printed in America. By Jonathan Benjamin. Northampton, Sept. 1799."

ORIGIN OF CHOIRS.

On the origin of choirs there is now very little
definite knowledge. The probability is that they
grew out of the organized efforts that followed the
Revolution of 1720 – 30. Singing societies had
been formed as early as 1720. These acted the
triple duty of agents to gather, and to diffuse
knowledge, and also to improve the style of performance. They were regularly organized singing
societies or schools. The natural tendency of
these combined efforts, was to collect, such as had
practised together during the week, into a group
to unite on the Sabbath. Hence the origin of
choirs in this country ; they grew out of circumstances. Those who had sung together, who
thought and who felt alike upon the great subject,
that had for years agitated almost every congregation in New England, would be very apt to seek
each other on the Sabbath, and thus form a choir

at once.   Schools too, had their influence in grouping the best singers, and uniting their influence and voices in the songs of the temple.   And the very spirit of opposition to regular singing, which had for many years existed, and which did exist for many years afterwards, being deeply seated in ignorance and prejudice, had its influence, in banding together those who had been so long, and so virulently opposed.

While there was much concerted action, there is no mention made of any regular choir, having separate seats, in any church for thirty or forty years.   And they certainly did not become common until near the time of the American Revolution.   If there were any choirs, they were doubtless to be found in Boston and its neighboring towns.   There were, without doubt, a few existing in the larger towns as early as 1750 ; and in some places, *perhaps* from the Revolution of 1720, but not in the country generally.   There were few country churches with a choir before 1765 or 70.   They were generally formed as the people could be induced to allow them ;   and in most places it was with no little trouble that permission was obtained.   In some parishes it was the constant labor of years ; but in others they were forced by some sudden emergency to yield at once.   They were generally formed as the custom of "lining out" the Psalm was done away. Or perhaps they were the means of removing that barbarous and penurious custom. At any rate, the choirs and that custom were ever at a war, in which the former have ever proved victorious.

The following records will serve to illustrate the time, the manner, and the trouble, of forming choirs; also, the importance attached to, and the manner of, choosing a leading singer.

" 1762. The parish voted, that those who had learned the art of singing may have liberty to sit in the front gallery. They did not take the liberty." Probably because they would not sing after the clerk's reading.

" 1780. The parish requested Jonathan Chaplin, Jr., and Lieutenant Spafford to assist Deacon Daniel Spafford in *Raising the tune* in the Meeting house."

" 1785. The parish desire the singers, both male and female, to sit in the gallery, and will allow them to sing once upon each Lord's day without reading by the Deacon."

" About 1790 the *lining out* the psalm or hymn by the deacons, was wholly discontinued."

History of Rowley, p. 93.

" 1764, Jan. 5. Voted, ' That the pastor be

desired, sabbath preceding the next lecture, in the name of the Church, to desire the congregation, after the lecture is over, to tarry and consult with the church about choosing some person, or persons, to set the psalm when Capt. Averill is absent.'

" 1764, March 13. Mr. Moses Perkins and Mr. Jacob Kimball, were, by the brethren of the church, and also by the congregation, chosen to set the psalm.

" Voted, ' That the said Perkins and Kimball set in the Elders seat.' "

Topsfield Church Records.

Topsfield is one of the oldest churches away from the seaboard ; and though famed for its many singers, the above votes render it almost certain, that they had no choir at that time ; but within five years after this, they had an efficient choir, sitting in the front gallery, the place assigned.

" 1773. The seats for the choir were designated by the First Parish in Ipswich, being ' two back on each side of the front alley.'

" Similar provision was made at the Hamlet, now Hamilton, in 1764, and at Chebacco in 1788. The choir of the First Parish began to sit in the gallery in 1781. This alteration was soon imitated in the other parishes."

Felt's History of Ipswich.

" At Worcester, Mass. in 1770, four men were chosen to lead the music on the Lord's day. These were to sit in the elder's seat. Three years after this, 1773, the first attempt at forming a choir was made ; and the two head seats on the men's side on the lower floor of the meeting house were assigned to those who sat together to conduct the singing.

" The final blow was struck to the old system by the resolution of the town, Aug. 5, 1779. Voted, That the singers sit in the front seats in the front gallery, and that those gentlemen who have hitherto, sat in the front seats in said gallery, have a right to sit in the front, and second seat below, and that said singers have said seats appropriated to said use. Voted, that said singers be requested to take said seats and carry on the singing in public worship. Voted, that the mode of singing in the congregation here, be without reading the psalms line by line to be sung.

" The Sabbath succeeding the adoption of these votes, after the hymn had been read by the minister, the aged and venerable Deacon Chamberlain, unwilling to desert the custom of his fathers, rose and read the first line according to the usual practice. The singers, prepared to carry the alteration into effect, proceeded without pausing at the con-

clusion.   The white-haired officer of the church,
with the full power of his voice read on, until the
louder notes of the collected body overpowered the
attempt to resist the progress of improvement, and
the deacon deeply mortified at the triumph of
musical reformation, seized his hat, and retired
from the meeting-house in tears.   His conduct
was censured by the church, and he was for a time
deprived of its communion, for absenting himself
from the public services of the Sabbath."

History of Worcester.

LINING OUT THE PSALM — A CONTROVERSY.

For some years before the time of the American
Revolution, a short, but exciting discussion was
carried on, in different places, at different times,
concerning reading the psalms and hymns, one or
two lines at a time, for the people to sing, or, as it
was called, " *lining out the psalm.*" This was a
short-lived contagion, that made its appearance
where, and whenever an attempt was made to
banish that custom, and which passed from one town
to another, until nearly all were infected by it.   In
some places, however, the discussion became a pro-
tracted disease ; preying steadily on the peace of
the church for five, ten, fifteen, and sometimes even
twenty years.   About the year 1750, the custom

of reading the lines had gained almost universal usage. It was first introduced by the churches in this country, as they changed their manuals of psalmody; Ainsworth's for the New England Version or Bay Psalm Book.

The custom of "lining out the psalm," probably had its origin with Metrical Psalmody; and that was contemporary with the Reformation. When the Reformers first composed their hymns, they would doubtless often desire to use them at once in their public services; and having no conveniences for printing them, they would take the only way left, poor and undesirable as it was, which would be, for one to parcel out the hymn, for the others to sing. This method, however, was only practised for a short time. Soon, printed manuals were found in plenty, in all the Protestant congregations; and even the Roman Catholics themselves were using them for a time. The Protestants generally either had books or else memorized the hymns, so that lining out was never much practised among them, until long after Protestantism was established.

When the Puritans first came to this country, it was their good custom to sing without reading the line; but when the Bay Psalm Book was introduced, a few congregations, in imitation of their

12

brethren in England, introduced the method of
reading the psalm line by line, for the people to
sing. This, at first, was by no means common;
but in the course of thirty or forty years, it became
the general custom, and so continued for nearly or
quite, one century. The custom was adopted by
the church in Plymouth in 1681, and probably by
some others about the same time.[1] In 1664, the
" Westminster Assembly " recommended to the
churches that were not supplied with books, to

---

[1] The following is an extract from the Plymouth Church Records.
" A church meeting was called by the Elder to be on Feb. 10, (1680.)
At this meeting the Elder told the church *a brother* earnestly desired
the Psalm might be read in public worship, because else he was in-
capable of practicing that ordinance ; the matter was much agitated ;
the Elder propounded to the church to speak man by man whether
they judged reading the Psalms in order to singing was lawful, and
that they could rest in the practice of it. The issue of the meeting
was, the church desired the pastor that he would in his public
preaching, hold forth from Scripture the lawfulness and necessity of
reading the Psalms, which he expressed his willingness and purpose
to do, and till then the practice of reading might be deferred.

"Sept. 18, 1681, the Pastor from Col. 3, 16, in preaching showed
the lawfulness and necessity of reading the Psalm in order to
singing.

" Oct 2, the Elder stayed the church and desired to know their
minds ; Some of the bretheren rather desired the old custom of not
reading might be continued ; but the body of the church declared for
the lawfulness of reading, and all would rest in the practice of it ;
accordingly Oct. 9th the Elder began to read the Psalm, and desired
the Pastor to expound the psalm before singing and the Pastor did
from that time constantly attend exposition throughout the whole
book of Psalms."

read their psalms and hymns line by line. The design of the recommendation was not for all churches to adopt it, but only for such as were unable to procure books. The indifference of the people soon brought the thing recommended into a general custom; and a scheme that was designed only to meet an emergency for the poor, to the great injury of the church, was adopted by all. In some churches, however, as Dr. Cotton Mather in his "Church Discipline" tells us; "The assembly being furnished with psalm books, they sing without the stop of reading between every line." The service of reading was generally performed by the elder, or one of the deacons, who was also called the clerk, yet sometimes by another person appointed by the pastor.

The first complaint of this custom found in print, was by the Rev. Dr. Watts, in the preface to an early edition of his psalms and hymns. This was seen by few, until that manual was introduced into the colonial churches; which was about the time of the American Revolution; some before, some after. The introduction of this work was the means of their acting upon the Doctor's good suggestions. In the preface he says:

"It were to be wished that all congregations and private families would sing as they do in foreign Protestant countries, without reading line by line. Though the author has done what he could to make the sense complete in every line or two ; yet many inconveniences will always attend this unhappy manner of singing. But where it cannot be altered, these two things may give some relief.

" First. Let as many as can do it, bring psalm books with them, and look on the words while they sing, so far as to make the sense complete.

" Secondly. Let the clerk read the whole psalm over aloud, before he begins to parcel out the lines ; that the people may have some notion of what they sing, and not be forced to drag on heavily through eight tedious syllables, without any meaning, until the next line comes to give the sense of them."

The attempt to put aside this " good old way," was most vehemently opposed by many, and in almost every town a hard contention took place. In some churches this was settled at once by the clergyman ; but in most a war of words and a virulence of feeling followed, that had not visited the congregations since the Reformation of 1720 – 30. By this change however, the church was not disturbed for any length of time ; a few hearty struggles, and those who defended " the good old way " yielded, and the " innovation " was established.

The choirs which had been, and were being organized, had no small hand in cutting short the difficulties, which otherwise might have been prolonged, much to the disturbance and injury of the church. In their zeal for performing that part of the public service, which they had either voluntarily, or by request taken upon themselves; and perhaps being, as choirs are too apt to be, of a restive disposition, they would either forget, or purposely sing on, without waiting for the deacon to read the line. This would bring down a tempest of indignation expressed, upon the choir, from the clerk and his friends, whose duty had been thus ruthlessly torn from him. The choir, of course, would be quite as promptly in their seats, and when singing, quite as prompt to *their time*, as though the people had been silent during the week. It would matter but little if the clerk should get the better of the choir, as they sometimes did, and set the tune; the choir could either set another, and in the fury of their strength, lead off in a march so resistless, that all, willing or not, would be obliged to follow, or sit silent; or deeming it best to humor the matter, join the clerk, and taking him and his tune on their impetuous current, bear them gallantly on in their own time and manner. An attempt to stop them to read the

line, when they had fully determined to go, would
be an attempt to stop the whirlwind in its course.
Hence a few efforts, and the clerk sat in hope-
less despair at their rashness and impiety. Here
and there an indignant clerk might be found who
would take his revenge on the spot, as once happened in the town of T., in Massachusetts. The
choir having led off with a little too much zeal,
without giving the deacon time to read, he rose at
the conclusion of the psalm, and gravely setting his
spectacles upon his nose, opened his book, saying:
" now let the people of God sing." He accordingly set a psalm, and in pity and respect to the
good old man, all joined in singing it.

HEDGE'S SERMON.

1772.   The following extract from a sermon, will
serve to show something of the state of feeling, and the principal arguments, both for and
against omitting to read the lines. This sermon
was " preached at a singing lecture in Warwick,
January 29, 1772. By Lemuel Hedge, A. M.,
pastor of the church there."

1772.   " The custom of reading the psalm, *line
by line*, as it is sung, is objected against, by
the greatest masters of song, as a violation of the
rules of singing. But so great are the advantages

that are supposed to accrue by that practice another
way, that many are loth to give it up: and this in
many places causes great heat and contention. I
shall not think it amiss at this time, briefly to consider this matter, and shall endeavour to give the
arguments on both sides, their due weight that we
may better come to the knowledge of our own
duty in this affair.

"As to matters of God's worship, we have
nothing to direct us therein but his *Word*, — or the
practice of the *primitive* Churches, — or the *expe-
diency* and *fitness* of things. — The Word of God
is the only rule of conscience; and no man can
say that he cant in conscience, comply with any
proposed practice, unless he can see something in
the Scriptures that forbids it. He may plead that
his humour forbids it, but he cant plead *conscience*,
unless he finds something in the Bible, that directs
him in the case. Now the Bible nowhere tells us,
that the psalm shall be read line by line when
we sing; nor is anything there said, that implies
any such thing. It is well known to all that have
looked into *antiquity*, and what was the custom of
the Jewish church, that they never practiced reading with singing. Indeed, their *tunes* were so
contrived, that they would not admit of such a

practice. They were something like our *anthems*,[1] musical notes were set over the words in their psalm-books, which directed their voices, as they pronounced the words in singing. Christ and his Apostles were trained up in this manner of singing, and were able to sing *together*, as we find they did at the institution of the Lord's Supper. They did not form a new *scale* of music, but kept to that which was practiced upon in the Jewish Church.

" As to the *Primitive Christians*, we find not the least tittle to incline us to think that reading with singing, was ever practiced in a single instance by *them ;* nor the least mention of any such officer as a *Reader* of the psalm for the congregation, when singing : and certainly it belonged not to the *Deacon's* office, any more than to the office of any one else, — and yet some of the writers of those times, professedly give an account of the *customs* and *practices* of christians in their public worship ; so that, if it had been the custom to *read* with *singing*, it is very unaccountable, that they should say nothing at all about it. And I believe I may safely challenge any man to produce a single instance, of thus reading with singing for about fifteen hundred years after Christ. I confess

[1] See Dr. Watts's larger Preface to his version of the Psalms, p. 17.

I am unable to give a particular account, how the practice came to take place in Christian churches : But the most probable conjecture is this. When a Reformation from Popery took place, the psalmody of the Church of *Rome* was so corrupted with popish doctrines and superstitions, that when the Reformers broke off from her communion, they left their psalm-books behind them ; and whenever a version was published according to the *Protestant scheme*, special care was taken by the Pope to suppress all *such* translations ; and in those countries where his influence most extended, very few such psalm-books could be procured : And as *ignorance* with them was the *mother of* devotion, very few were taught to read, and so, unable to make use of psalm-books if they had them. So that the churches were obliged either to alter the *manner* of their singing, or many of them lose the *matter* of the song. For which reason it was probable they first allowed of reading with singing. But it appears that this practice never took place in *most* of the Reformed Churches." . . . .

" Thus those who are in favour of singing without reading plead — that they have the example of God's ancient church — the practice of Christ and his Apostles, and of the Christian church for fifteen hundred years together — that reading is a violation of the rules of singing — interrupts the song — hurts the melody and disappoints them of the pleasure of the music — that in a country where psalm-books may be had at so cheap a rate, as among us, it is entirely needless to have it so — and if people would provide themselves with *books* (as they ought to do) they would better take the sense, and see the connection of one line and verse, with another, than they possibly can do by hearing it read line by line — all might better understand the *matter* of the song, and no interruption given to the *manner* of it.

" But on the other side it is plead — That many people are poor, and unable to purchase psalm-books — that others are old, and unable to see to read if they had them — that there are many young people and others, that cant so well read, and they would take the sense much better to have it read line by line : They plead also — that it has always been the practice of our Fore-fathers in this Land — and that this singing without reading, is a new-found invention of man — that it disturbs the peace of Churches and Societies — and (those that know no better will say that it) is a leading step to *popery ;* and that if they once begin to let in new things, they know not where they shall stop — and that since they have reason to believe that God has heard the prayers, and accepted the praises of his people in this land, when they have worshipped him in the manner they now do — and since also, they cannot see that *reading* does give such an interruption to regular singing as is pretended ; — they cant see their way clear to encourage the practice of singing without it ; — It is what they never heard of till late, and they dont love to be given to change. These are their main objections. Let us consider them and see what can be said in answer to them.

" As to people's being poor, and unable to purchace psalm-books ; there are enough that will engage to *give* to such as are not able to buy for themselves ; so that this objection is quickly answered.

" As to those that cannot *see* to read, or cannot *read* if they could see ; doubtless reading line by line may be of some advantage to them ; but I presume the number of such is very small, — and there may be others that are *deaf*, and cannot hear, if it is read ; and yet because it is not customary to carry psalm-books to public worship, they neglect it, for fear of being looked upon as singular, and making their infirmity to be taken notice of by the assembly : Whereas if it had been customary to carry *books* (as it would have been if there had been no reading) they would have done it, and so, would always have been able to have taken the sense of the psalm as it was sung. But further — considering the disadvantages that attend singing with reading, it may justly be questioned, whether for the sake of a *very few* old people, and persons that cannot read, congregations are in duty bound to tolerate that practice : We know of no such provision that was made for their infirmities, either in God's ancient Church, or by Christ and his Apostles, or by any of the primitive Churches : And if *they* did not, it will be hard to prove that we are in duty bound to do it. I would condescend as far for the sake of such, as is any way reasonable or convenient, but to do it at the expense of the regular performance of that part of worship, and to the disadvantage of so many others, is what I cannot see sufficient reason for. Besides, when once those persons become better acquainted with the method, they will by the help of hearing the psalm once read over by the *minister*, and attending to the *singers* as it is sung, (if they speak the words as distinctly and plainly as they can, which they should be careful to do) I say such persons, and indeed all the congregation may understand most that is sung. So that *reading* with singing will be but of very little, if any advantage upon this account.

" As to the plea that it has been the *universal practice*, of our *Forefathers* in this land, and that to sing without reading, is a *new-found invention of man ;* this is wholly a mistake. — MR. MATHER in his *Ratio Disciplinæ*, a book published above fifty years ago, tells us, 'that some congregations, where they had psalm books sung *without reading ;* ' and it is well known to those who have made due enquiry, that it was never practiced in some of the *oldest* churches in this land ; and it is so far from being a new invention, that it is as old as christianity itself, and was the method practiced by our Savior and his Apostles : So that when we plead for it, we ask for no more, than what was the *good old way* — and it is to be hoped that all who are lovers of that way will readily join with us.

" As for making *disturbances* in the church — it is generally observed that those who are most disturbed, are commonly such as know the least of the matter. There is no reformation that is ever set on foot, even though it be from such gross corruptions as Idolatry itself, but what will cause disturbances, and breed contention. The ignorance of some, the prejudice of others, and the wilfulness of more, will always raise opposition. And what ? because of this shall we never attempt to reform ?

We were unworthy the name of Christians if we did not. Indeed in matters of little or no consequence, it is not worth while to disturb the peace of societies about them : And whether the thing now pleaded for, be worth *contending* about, I will not determine — I hope none are for driving matters to extremity, or making such a point of it, as to disturb the peace of society : — But then, *one* way, or the *other* may be most agreeable to the body of the people, and most acceptable to God ; and it cannot be amiss to consider what may be said on both sides of the question. And I hope that every one will judge for *himself*, and act upon that side where he sees the greatest light.

"As to its being a leading step to *popery* and an inlet to innovations ; there is not the least foundation for such an assertion. This is only the 'Bug-bear of folly,' and an outcry to disturb the minds of others. For what sort of connection can any one see, between singing without reading and popery ? They may as well say that the practice of primitive christianity led to *popery*. And if it is really a reformation in our worship, to sing without reading, and a coming nearer to primitive christians, we ought to rejoice in it, and be glad of *such* innovations every day.

"Doubtless God has heard the prayers, and

accepted the praises of his people in this land, though they have not sung in the manner that is here pleaded for. It is not every irregular practice in his worship that will cause *him* who is infinite in mercy, and ready to pardon, to reject the prayers and praises of his worshippers. But although He has accepted the praises of his people when performed in a less suitable manner, it will not from thence follow, that they would not have been more acceptable, if they had been performed in a different manner: And therefore it can be no plea for continuing *that* practice. Though the prayers and praises of a person not perfectly sanctified, may be acceptable to God ; yet it would be very wicked for a person to say — that therefore he will not press forward towards greater perfection ; for certainly the nearer he gets to perfection, the better he performs his duty, and the more acceptable to God.

" These are the main pleas that are made in favour of the present customary way of singing — *you yourselves*, are to judge of the force of them, and of the answers given to them."

Such were the objections, and such the answers that were a thousand times made during this discussion. The light that was thrown upon the matter during this controversy, and the success of the experiment, assured the people that they might alter some things for the better, without either breaking up their church or marring their religion. It taught them that prejudice alone hindered them, and that removed, they had one interesting exercise of their public worship, purified, brightened and rendered a thousandfold more interesting.

But it gained not the whole ground. While it removed this nuisance of public worship, from many churches, it left untouched by far the greater number. It had operated only upon a small part of New England, while the custom was still retained over all the remaining part of the States. But it had removed the prejudice that lay as a spell upon the churches, and they were left free to act as they might think best. From that time to the present, the churches have been laying aside that custom, from time to time, as they could be brought to feel that they were rich enough, or careful enough to obtain books. Yet still, to this day, it prevails over three-fourths of the territory of the United States. In some churches it is wholly used, and in others, only in their more social meetings. And still may be heard the same perplexities, that must always be found where this custom prevails — its broken and retarded sense, and its spoiled melody. Still may be heard occa-

sional incongruities, as absurd, as those recorded
of our fathers, when they read, and gravely sang:

" The Lord will come, and he will not " —

and pursuing the contradiction to a climax of ab-
surdity, read and sang on :

" Keep silence, but speak out."

It is but a year or two, since the writer frequently attended church, in one of the western
states, where the clerk, a lawyer of some note,
used to dole out the hymn two lines at a time —
with a nasal twang that Ichabod Crane might have
coveted, but could never have obtained — always
having the good fortune to be able to run out of
the tune into the words, and from the words into
the tune, without stopping or changing either the
pitch or time.

Ignorance and thoughtlessness alone retain the
custom ; and, as they are dissipated by proper
knowledge, this custom, so obnoxious to good
music, will also disappear.

13

BIOGRAPHICAL SKETCHES.

REFORMERS.

REV. JOHN COTTON.

When God, in his wisdom, sees it necessary to perform any great work for his church, he always, and amply provides the agents and the means by which to accomplish it. When the moral darkness and error, that, like some dark spirit had brooded over the church for centuries, was to be dissipated, then Luther, the orator and logician, was raised up to confute and to persuade ; and, as with the fate of the church resting upon his action, he stood forth a moral and sublime conqueror of the powers of corruption and darkness. For religious liberty, Luther wielded an argument, and Cromwell a sword. When the church to be more pure, and to be prepared for the latter-day glory, must be transplanted to the American wilds, then were raised up men able to lead the pilgrim bands, to teach those lessons of wisdom, and to implant those principles of eternal justice and truth, that should make a handful of pilgrims become a host, a light to the world, and a manifestation of God's special presence. Among these were men like Cotton, Norton, Wilson, Davenport, Hooker and others.

John Cotton was born at the town of Derby, England, December 4th, 1585 ; and died at Boston, in the Massachusetts colony, October 23d, 1652. He was of an honorable family ; yet it was not the blood of his progenitors, but the grace and goodness of God, that made him truly noble. His father, Roland Cotton, was by profession a lawyer. The family had been deprived of great revenues, and Roland Cotton was thus educated by his friends, that he might be better prepared to recover the estate.

The parents of John Cotton were both eminently pious, and sought rather to make their child a Christian, than a great man. Towards the latter, however, nature had done so much, that art could scarcely fail. He was early placed at school, and so great was his proficiency, that he was considered quite a prodigy. Luther was made A. M. at the age of *twenty*, Melancthon A. B. at *fourteen*, but Cotton received his first honor at *thirteen*.

Soon after he finished his course of study, at

Trinity College, he was made Professor at Eman-
uel College, and at no distant period, became the
principal *Lecturer, Catechist,* and *Dean* of that
Institution.   While there, he pronounced several
brilliant and masterly orations, that gave him great
reputation in the University.   His sermons before
the University were greatly admired — he was a
scholar, a wit, and an orator — " and that which
added unto his Reputation, was, an *University
Sermon,* wherein *Aiming* more to Preach *Self,*
than *Christ,* he used such *Florid Strains,* as ex-
tremely Recommended him unto *the most* who
Relished the *Wisdom of words,* above the *Words
of Wisdom :* though the Pompous Eloquence of
that Sermon, afterwards gave such a Distaste unto
his own *Renewed Soul,* that with a sacred indignation he threw his Notes into the Fire."

Cotton Mather.

Mr. Cotton preached for some years before he
experienced that change of heart which is the first
requisite for a true ambassador of Christ.   He was
first impressed with the necessity of personal, vital
religion, while young, under the preaching of the
celebrated William Perkins ; but would not listen
to the voice that called " return ; " and even when
that good and great man died, he rejoiced in his
deliverance from that powerful ministry.   But after

his conversion, he bitterly repented of these wicked feelings. He was at last awakened by hearing a sermon from Dr. Sibs, on the misery of those who have but a negative righteousness. This was the means of turning not only his heart towards vital religion, but his whole course of action, for life. From this time, he preached Christ and him crucified. But it cost him his fame at the University. The Wits and Scholars were unwilling to hear the truth, and the Vice Chancellor no longer offered him the hand of friendship.

At this stage of affairs in the University, the people of Boston, Lincolnshire, England, invited him to become their minister, which invitation he accepted ; and there he labored to destroy the leaven of Arminianism, and to encourage holy living, with signal success.

After he had preached about three years at Bos ton, he was brought to feel that there were many evils unreformed in the Church of England ; and from that time he became a conscientious Non Conformist ; and such was his influence over his people, that a greater part of the town embraced his views. For this, Mr. Cotton was silenced ; but was soon offered, on condition of his conforming, not only liberty to preach, but also a high prefer-

ment.   He was not, however, to be tempted to
violate his conscience by such inducements, but
stood inflexibly a Non Conformist to the day of his
death.

Mr. Cotton's standing, influence, power, meekness and discretion, soon freed him from a persecution, which under other circumstances, would
have increased.   He was restored to the ministry
by means of the very individual who had complained of him.   The storm of persecution passed
off, and he was permitted to pursue his labors in
his own way for some years.   During this time, he
was engaged not in making proselytes to this, or
that party, but in preaching faithfully, and fer-
vently the great doctrines of Christianity.

After an active and signally useful ministry of
twenty years at Boston, the Demon, Persecution,
again molested him.   He was summoned before
the High Commissioner's Court ; but knowing if
he appeared there, the offence of Non Conformity
would be clearly proved against him, and he im-
prisoned, he concealed himself from his foes.
While in this state of concealment, in hope of
being again pardoned, the Archbishop sent word
to him, " that if he had been guilty of Drunken-
ness or Uncleanness or any such *Lesser-fault*, he
could have obtained his Pardon ; but inasmuch as

he had been Guilty of *Non Conformity* and *Puritanism*, the Crime was unpardonable ; and therefore said he, ' *You must Fly for your Safety.* ' "
He at once under an assumed name and dress, fled with the full purpose of going to Holland. On his way his attention was turned to London, and thither he went. There he found several distinguished clergymen, who thought the imposed ceremonies, indifferent and sufferable trifles. These, being sorry that he had left Boston, and that he was about to leave his country, proposed a conference, to which Mr. Cotton readily consented. The debate ended in their full and complete conversion to his opinions and practices ; and it gave to New England the distinguished men, Dr. Goodwin, Mr. Nye, and Mr. Davenport, besides leaving several acute and accomplished men as Non Conformists in London.

Mr. Cotton, fearing to remain at London, soon took ship to America, where he immediately entered upon the great work the Lord had assigned him. He was now quiet in the possession of his principles, with none to molest or make afraid. Here, as pastor of the first church in Boston, he quietly pursued his work, while his fame at every step, was heard, and echoed back from the Halls of England. In 1641, " some Great Persons in

England, were intending to have sent over a
Ship, on purpose to fetch him over, for the sake of
the Service, that such a Man as *He,* might then
Do to the Church of God, then, *Travelling* in the
Nation.   But although their Doubt of his *Willing-
ness to Remove* caused them to forbear that
Method of obtaining him, yet the Principal Mem-
bers, in both Houses of *Parliament,* wrote unto
him, with an Importunity for his Return into
England ; which had prevailed with him, if the
Dismal Showres of *Blood,* quickly after breaking
upon the Nation, had not made such Afflictive
Impressions upon him, as to prevent his purpose.
He continued, therefore, in *Boston,* unto his
Dying Day ; Counting it a great Favour of
Heaven unto him, that he was Delivered from *the
Unsettledness of Habitation,* which was not
among the least of the Calamities, that Exercised
the Apostles of our Lord.   *Nineteen Years* and
odd Months, he spent in this Place, doing of *Good*
Publickly and Privately, unto all sorts of men, as it
became *a Good Man full of Faith, and of the
Holy Ghost."   Cotton Mather.*

Eleven years did this eminent servant of God
labor with his church, and for the good of the
Colonies, after he refused to return.   But now his
time had arrived.   As he was going over to

Cambridge to preach, he was wet in crossing the ferry. An inflammation of the lungs was the result, from which he never entirely recovered, though he was able, subsequently, to preach twice to his people, before he was finally called to his rest.

While he lay sick, the people — the magistrates — all, came to receive instruction, and a blessing from his lips. Among others, that noted man, President Dunster, of Cambridge College, came, and with tears in his eyes, asked his blessing, saying : " *I know in my heart, they whom you bless, shall be blessed.*" Just before his death, he sent for the Elders of his church, in accordance with the Apostolic injunction, to pray over him ; and then he exhorted them in the most earnest manner, faithfully to feed his flock. He was then just ready for his departure, when Mr. Wilson, his colleague, coming in to take his leave, expressed the wish, that God might lift up the light of his countenance upon him, to which he instantly replied ; " God hath done it already, Brother ! " He called for his children, commended them to his God, and then desired to be left alone to prepare for the approaching hour ; and thus, after lying speechless a few hours, he was no more, for God took him !

Mr. Cotton was twice married, and had three sons and three daughters. Two sons he left distinguished in the ministry, and the third died while preparing for that high vocation. He also had five grand-sons in that holy calling ; of whom the honored Cotton Mather was one.

He was a great man, an humble Christian, and a faithful laborer in his Master's service. He preached and wrote, as though he felt it his business to instruct ; doing things worthy to be written, and writing things worthy to be read. So great were his labors, and so systematic, that there was no text of the whole Bible left unexplained to his people. As a public man, he was consulted both in church and state ; and on the judgment of few men could more implicit reliance be placed. His famous work, " The Keys," was the first work published upon the Congregational church government ; and was always esteemed as second only to the " Platform of Church Discipline," published at Cambridge, in 1648.

He was a hard student. " Mr. Cotton was indeed a most *Universal Scholar*, a *Living System* of the Liberal Arts, and a *Walking Library*." While he was a *critic* in the Greek, he *conversed* in the Latin and Hebrew. As a preacher, he was animated, but dignified, learned and profound ;

never showing himself, but his subject; and his humble, diligent, faithful labors were greatly blessed.

In his personal appearance, " he was of a Clear, Fair, Sanguine Complection, and like *David* of *Ruddy Countenance.* He was rather *Low* than *Tall*, and rather *Fat* than *Lean;* but of a Becoming *Mediocrity.* In his Younger years, his Hair was *Brown*, but in his Latter years, as *White*, as the Driven Snow. In his Countenance there was an Inexpressible sort of Majesty, which Commanded Reverence from all that approached him; This Cotton was indeed the *Cato* of his Age, for his Gravity, but had a Glory with it which *Cato* had not." *Cotton Mather.*

Mr. Cotton's acquaintance was with such men as Perkins, Ames, Hildersham, Dodd, Drs. Preston, Twiss and Owen, and Archbishop Williams.

In his life he was greatly honored, and in his death sincerely lamented. He lived a life of remarkable usefulness, and died full of the hopes of a blessed immortality.

REV. THOMAS SYMMES, D. D.

Rev. Thomas Symmes, of Bradford, Mass., the son of Rev. Zechariah Symmes, the first minister of that place, was born at Bradford, February 1st,

1678. In 1698, he was graduated at Harvard College: and was settled over the church in Boxford, December 30th, 1702. He continued in charge of that church and people, until 1708; when, shortly after his father's death, he was dismissed from the church in Boxford, and immediately succeeded to his father's charge in Bradford.

Mr. Symmes possessed strong powers of mind; which being united with great learning, independence, and energy of character, rendered him a man of great influence in society. In the pulpit, he was animated, popular and faithful; and his exertions for the spiritual welfare of his flock were crowned, at various times, with great accessions to his church.

Mr. Symmes's musical writings were of great importance at the time they were circulated, and not less so at this day, as historical matter.[1] It is to be regretted that they had not possessed a greater share of the meekness that characterized other writers in that discussion. He seemed to have no forbearance with the whims, ignorance, and prejudice of the people, and dealt out satirical

[1] He wrote three musical tracts. The first was entitled "The Reasonableness of Regular Singing: or Singing by Note;" 1720. The second, "Prejudice in Matters of Religion," 1722 The third "Uteli Dulci: or Joco-Serious Dialogue," 1723.

argument with a vehemence that showed the energy, if not the meekness, of his character. After a short, but useful life, he died at Bradford, October 6th, 1725, aged forty-eight years.

REV. SOLOMON STODDARD.

Mr. Stoddard was born of a noble family, at Boston, Mass., in 1643. In 1662, he was graduated at Cambridge College, where he remained in connection with the college about eight years ; and subsequently, for two years, he was preaching to the dissenters, on the island of Barbadoes. September 11th, 1672, he was ordained as successor to Rev. Eleazer Mather, over the church in Northampton ; where he continued until his death, February 11th, 1729, in the eighty-sixth year of his age, having been settled over the same people fifty-seven years.

Mr. Stoddard's sermons, theological essays, and controversial writings, gave him uncommon distinction. He was a learned man, and an acute disputant. In the pulpit, he was " plain, experimental, searching and argumentative ; " and his labors were blessed by a remarkable ingathering of souls. Under his ministration, there were five great revivals of religion. The first, in 1679 ; the second, in 1683 ; the third, 1696 ; the fourth, 1712 ; the fifth, 1718. In each of these, the people generally were greatly concerned for their eternal salvation.

He entered into the controversy on the subject of regular singing, with his accustomed energy. For this he wrote, in 1722, one essay, called "Cases of Conscience;" and published one sermon, "to stir up young men and maidens to praise the Lord." Few men of his day held a more commanding influence, or a more unblemished reputation.

REV. PETER THACHER.

Rev. Peter Thacher, whose name stands connected with the two Mr. Danforths, in the "Cases of Conscience," might have been either of three eminent men, of the same name, living at that time, in the Massachusetts Colony. Either would have been an honor to any party of men that could have been brought together. They were men of sound minds, great learning, and ardent piety, as were all who engaged in the Musical Revolution of 1720 – 30. If it was Mr. Thacher of Boston, as is most likely, that document was graced with a name the colony might be justly proud to own.

REV. JOHN DANFORTH.

This excellent man, though not wanting in

learning or genius, was more eminent for the clergyman's best qualification, piety. In him the scholar, the christian, the pastor, and the teacher, found a pattern of uncommon perfection. He had attained great knowledge in the mathematics, and also possessed quite a poetic talent. Mr. Danforth was graduated at Harvard, in 1677; became pastor of the church in Dorchester, in 1682, and continued in his useful ministry, until May 26th, 1730, when he fell asleep, and was gathered to his fathers.

REV. SAMUEL DANFORTH.

Mr. Danforth " was one of the most learned and eminent ministers of his day ; " and one of the many worthies, whose labors were so greatly blessed by the rich outpouring of the Holy Spirit. About the year 1705, his church enjoyed a remarkable revival of religion, in which the youth were converted in great numbers. He was born at Roxbury, December, 18th, 1666; was a graduate of Harvard, in 1683 ; and died November 14th, 1727.

REV. NATHANIEL CHAUNCEY.

This clergyman, settled in Durham, Ct., was a son of the Rev. Israel Chauncey, and grandson of

Rev. Charles Chauncey, second president of Harvard College. He was educated in Connecticut; and was the first person on whom the honors of Yale College were conferred. " Through life, he was regarded as a man of wisdom and prudence ; as a good scholar, and as an able divine." In the spring and summer of 1736, Mr. Chauncey's labors were attended by a remarkable revival of religion, in which there was no small ingathering of souls. His sermons were written and committed to memory, so that he used no manuscript when preaching. " His elocution was distinct, and his address grave and pungent. In his family and among his people, in all the relations and duties of life, his conduct was such as becomes the Gospel. After a ministry of almost fifty years, he descended to the grave, greatly lamented."

In the above sketches, we have shown something of the character and standing of the men who took part in the discussions concerning " Regular Singing." Never was a discussion in this country conducted by better men, or men of better minds. Of all, who either wrote or indorsed the pamphlets on that discussion, only *four* of *twenty* have not found a place among the worthies of New England, in the Biographical Dictionaries ; and only *one* of

the *writers*, Mr. Chauncey of Connecticut, is over-
looked. They were, generally, clergymen of the
most enlightened minds and ardent piety. Should
they be called weak because they were interested
for the music of the church ? They were the men
upon whom rested the labor, and the defence of
the church and her doctrines; and they have
rarely rested in better hands. There was Sewall,
humble, deliberate, cautious, and courageous;
fearing nothing but sin : And Prince, the learned
and refined; the faithful pastor and the able an-
nalist : And Cooper, the amiable, lovely friend;
the practical, evangelical, solemn, and eminently
successful preacher : And Foxcroft, the learned
divine, the pungent speaker, and the good Christian : And Mather, the dignified and accomplished
gentleman, the patriot and philanthropist, the ripe
scholar, and the pious and faithful pastor: And
Walter, the affectionate friend, the profound rea-
soner, and the eminently pious man : And Wadsworth, the wise and prudent citizen, the luminous
and pathetic preacher : And Coleman, the amiable
and venerable man; the graceful and persuasive
orator, the useful citizen, the friend of man, and
the child of God. Of these, Dr. Increase Mather
and Mr. Wadsworth, were revered presidents of
Harvard College; and three, Messrs. Joseph

14

Sewall, William Cooper, and Benjamin Colman, were elected to that office, but did not accept. These were the men who lent their influence for the cultivation of music ; and with such a precedent, shall men now fear or feel ashamed to lend their influence to improve the songs of Zion ? Is there not a criminal neglect of duty, upon the subject, by ministers of the gospel, as well as by others ? Let our dignified clergy take a deep and abiding interest in our sacred music, and it shall no longer fail for want of strength.

AMERICAN PSALMISTS.

In England, Mr. Holland has done the noble work of snatching the memory of their Psalmists from unmerited neglect, by embodying a sketch of their life with a specimen of their poetry, in two handsome octavo volumes. In this country, no one has appeared to pay a similar tribute of respect to the memory of our Psalmists; yet, while we have not so many, we have those who stand in the first place of honor and excellence. Such are the translators of the Bay Psalm Book. This indeed is the only work of high reputation that has been made in America; yet we have had several others that have held no mean place in this department of sacred literature.

We propose, in imitation of Mr. Holland, to give a short sketch of some of our Psalmists, and also a specimen of their poetry, so far as we can.

Before introducing the American Psalmists, we

will give a brief sketch of the Author of the Manual of Psalmody, used by the Puritans when they came to this country.

HENRY AINSWORTH.

" A very learned man he was, and a close student, which much impaired his health. We have heard some, eminent in the knowledge of the tongues, of the University of Leyden, say, that they thought he had not his better for the Hebrew tongue in the University, nor scarce in Europe. He was a man, very modest, amiable, and social, in his ordinary course and carriage, of an innocent and unblameable life and conversation, of a meek spirit and a calm temper, void of passion, and not easily provoked. And yet he would be something smart, in his style to his opposers, in his public writings; at which we, that have seen his constant carriage, both in public disputes and the managing all church affairs, and such like occurrences, have sometimes marvelled. He had an excellent gift of teaching and opening the Scriptures ; and things did flow from him with that facility, plainness and sweetness, as did much affect his hearers. He was powerful and profound in doctrine, although his voice was not strong ; and had this excellency above many, that he was most ready and pregnant in the Scriptures, as if the book of God had been written in his heart; being as ready in his quotations, without tossing or turning his book, as if they had laid open before his eyes, and seldom missing a word in citing of any place, teaching not only the word and doctrine of God, but in the words of God, and for the most part in a continued phrase and words of Scripture. He used great dexterity, and was ready in comparing Scripture with Scripture, one with another. In a word, the times and place in which he lived were not worthy of such a man." [1]

This Rabbi of his age, as he was called, was the author of a very learned commentary on the five books of Moses, in which he shows himself a complete master of the oriental languages, and of the Jewish antiquities. For some years, he was teacher of the church at Amsterdam. His death was sudden, and not without suspicion of violence.

JOHN ELLIOT.

Amid the excitements and hurry of the present age, we are too prone to neglect the memory of great and good men of other days, and the lessons of wisdom illustrated in their lives. But a few

[1] Young's Chronicles of the Pilgrims.

scores of years, or even centuries, should not destroy our interest in their history, especially when intimately connected with the youth of our country. Yet how seldom are those worthies mentioned, who in the infancy of the American colonies, laid the foundations of whatever is most valuable in our institutions! Few have been the points of time when the church and the world were blessed with so many worthy and excellent men. Among the number, the subject of this brief sketch holds an honored preëminence.

John Elliot was born in England, in the year 1604, and died in the Massachusetts colony, in 1690, aged eighty-six years. Early in life, he was brought to a knowledge of the truth as it is in Christ, through the instrumentality of the excellent Hooker; and his acquaintance with him, contributed not a little to establish, if not to implant, those principles of action, that made him such a bright and shining light. He was educated in Cambridge University, England, and for a time, after leaving College, owing to difficulties in the way of Puritan clergymen, he was forced to seek employment as a schoolmaster. But he acted not long in that capacity. Just at that time, the tide of emigration was setting towards the new world. Hundreds of Puritans were transporting themselves, their fami-

lies, and interests to this land, then so full of all
that could fill the most romantic and enterprising
mind. Here, too, was a field for the most devout
and active Christian, where he might labor among
his friends, or for the good of the sons of the
forest. The devout, burning, enterprising Elliot,
was not long in determining his course. He
quickly enrolled himself among the valiant soldiers
of the cross, and braved the dangers of the ocean,
to live with those who had gone before, undis-
turbed, though in a wilderness, and among
savages.

On his arrival, in 1631, he united with the
church in Boston. Mr. Wilson, the pastor, having
returned to England to settle his affairs, Mr. Elliot
officiated during his absence. Upon Mr. Wilson's
return to this country, the people, having become
greatly attached to Mr. Elliot, were anxious to settle him, as Mr. Wilson's colleague. But, having
promised some of his friends in England, that
if they would emigrate to this country, he would
give himself to their service, he refused. In 1632,
these pious friends came to this country, and chose
their habitation near Boston, calling it Roxbury.
Here a church was soon constituted, and Mr.
Elliot became their pastor, and continued in that
relation for *almost threescore years !*

No sooner had he settled in his new relation, than he began a course of systematic preparation for preaching to, and instructing the poor natives, and, in a short time, he was enabled to commence his labors. His feelings were all alive to their interests, he had their entire confidence, he labored in prayer and faith, and soon saw his labors attended with the most pleasing and blessed results.

Mr. Elliot was a hard worker. In his labors he was persevering, in proportion as they were various and pressing. Few men have accomplished more, or have toiled in a more unostentatious manner. To the important and increasing church at Roxbury, his ministrations were regular and efficient. With the Indians he labored day by day, counting hunger and cold as nothing. Passing from hut to hut, in the driving rain, or burning sun of summer, or the sleet and snow of winter; resting himself on the ground by the wigwam fire, and partaking of their homely fare, he taught and exhorted, unmindful of his toil and exposure, if thus he might reclaim the poor wretches from their demon worship.

But his study, as well as the field, wood, and church, told of his earnest labors for the good of others. There he labored, not only to prepare for the pulpit and the field, but to speak, by the press, to millions who could never hear his voice. And in this department, his efforts were great and important. Soon after he came to this country, on account of his acquaintance with Hebrew, and his poetic talent, he was appointed, as one of three, to translate the book of Psalms into English metre, for the use of the New England churches. This important work, with the Rev. Messrs. Mather and Weld, he entered upon with great zeal, and accomplished it with remarkable despatch and ability. He also translated the whole Bible[1] into the Indian language, and prepared the Psalms in Indian verse, to be used as a manual of psalmody in their churches. Besides this, he translated several treatises of practical divinity, catechisms, and school books for their use, and wrote several books for the colonial churches.

He had *four* Indian congregations, to each of which he preached *once* every two weeks, until old age disabled him. He was aided in his ministry to the Indians, by native teachers and preachers, who labored all their time under his supervision and instruction. Beside these, there were, at the time of his death, in that part of New England, *six* churches of baptized Indians, and

---

[1] Mr. Elliot wrote out the whole translation with a single pen.

eighteen assemblies of catechumens, professing the
name of Christ.   There were also, at that time,
twenty-four Indian, and *four* English ministers,
who preached in the Indian language.   Some of
the Indian ministers were educated at Cambridge,
and were truly godly and capable teachers.   The
children, as well as adults, committed to memory,
and had explained to them, either the catechism by
the famous William Perkins, or that by the Westminster Assembly.   The latter was entirely memorized by many of the children.

In his habits, Mr. Elliot was regular and simple.
He never indulged his appetite with dainties, or
inflamed his head with wine.   He would lift up
his hands, and praise God for the variety and rich-
ness of a feast, but partake of only one plain dish.
When urged to drink wine, he would exclaim,
" Wine is a noble, generous liquor, and we should
be humbly thankful for it, but, as I remember,
water was made before it."   Thus he preserved a
clear head and strong health for the work that was
near his heart, and in this he labored unceasingly,
amid hardships and discouragements, that might
have borne down a thousand less determined, and
less trusting the promises of God.

Elliot was a man of true charity.   No object of
suffering ever met his eye that did not reach his

heart. He gave away even his necessaries. The poor counted him their father, and turned to him with filial confidence for relief. Nor was he satisfied with what HE could give, but would press his neighbors, with the most urgent importunity, to join with him in relieving the suffering poor. And in this work of love, his wife was a helpmeet indeed. She was a well-educated English lady, and had acquired a good knowledge of medicine and chirurgery, which enabled them not only to relieve the wants of the poor, but their infirmities also. Thus they went about, an angel pair, gaining great consolation and pleasure by exchanging their labors and money for the gratitude of their fellow men, and the blessing of their God.

He was a peace-maker. If he heard one complain of another, he would say, " Brother, learn the meaning of these three little words, *Bear, Forbear, Forgive.*" He would almost sacrifice right to peace. When there was once laid before him, in council, a bundle of papers containing the matter of difficulty between some people, he hastily threw them all into the fire, and with a glow brighter than the flame, exclaimed, "Brethren, wonder not at what I have done ; I did it on my knees this morning before I came before you." Blessed are the peace-makers, for they shall be called the children of God.

He was a man of fervent and uniform piety ; a
man of prayer, pure, frequent, fervent prayer.
He was constantly in the habit of sending up ejac-
ulatory petitions. They were his breath and his
life. By them he bespoke blessings for every person and affair with which he was connected. His
days of fasting and prayer were frequent and
solemn. Always, if he had any great difficulty or
trouble, he sought relief by a special season, saying, "If we have any great thing to be accomplished, it is best to work by an engine the world
sees not." He could say on his death-bed, "I
thank God I have loved fasting and prayer with all
my heart." And he not only kept his own heart
in a prayerful frame, but was continually kindling
the same hallowed fire in the hearts of others. If
any important news was told him, he would at
once propose prayer, that he might pour out his
gratitude and praise, or humbly seek for mercy.
As he visited among his people, or acquaintances,
he would say, "Come, let us not have a visit without a prayer; let us pray down the blessing of
heaven upon your family before we go." In the
society of ministers he would say, "Brethren, the
Lord Jesus takes much notice of what is done
among his ministers when they are together ; come,
let us pray before we part." He imposed it as a

law upon himself, that he would leave something of religion, of heaven, and of God, upon the minds of all with whom he met; hence his presence was always revered, and his lips, soon unsealed, like Mary's box of ointment, filled the room with a precious odor. He was also remarkable for his strict observance of the Sabbath. On this subject he had no laxness of principle to justify bad practices. He made it, not like many in these times, a free and easy, or a listless and idle day, but one in which he served his God, as vigorously as he served the world on week days. His motto was, "Bad Sabbaths make bad Christians," and so he labored during the Sabbath to obtain an unction that should go with him through the week.

It has been the lot of few men to live a longer or a more useful life, than the beloved and renowned Elliot, and it is rare we find one so industrious, so vigorous, so great, and so unpretending. His was a life of self-denial and toil — of patience and humility. With great success, and influence unelated — with great trials and difficulties, not discouraged, he pursued his plans with his eye steadily fixed upon the good of his fellow men and the glory of God, unmindful of the smiles or the frowns of men; "like ships at sea, while in, above the world."

As he drew near to the time of his departure, he was much in conversation with his friends about the great change. But there was no fear, or but one, which was truly pleasing and beautiful. He had two dear friends long passed into heaven before him — his old neighbors, Cotton, of Boston, and Mather, of Dorchester — these he often feared would wait for him, and conclude " he had gone the wrong way." He had no other fear. He had " fought the good fight " — he had " finished " his " course." Just before he was taken from the world, a friend, Rev. Nehemiah Walter, his colleague, coming in to see him, he said, " Brother, thou art welcome to my soul. Pray, retire to my study for me, and give me leave to be gone." Being fully aware that he was then about to enter upon his eternal rest, he exclaimed, " Welcome joy," and, in true keeping with his life, turned to his friends, and breathed, with his last breath, the exhortation, " *Pray*, PRAY, PRAY ! "

We can select no part of the Bay Psalms and say, " Mr. Elliot translated this," as can be done with Sternhold and Hopkins, or with Clement Marot and Theodor De Beza's versions ; and we regret that the portions translated by each, have not been recorded. We will therefore introduce the biographical sketches of the individuals, and refer the reader to the examples already given.

REV. THOMAS WELDE.

" Thomas Welde, first minister of Roxbury, Mass., a native of England, was a minister in Essex before he came to this country. Refusing to comply with the impositions of the established church, he determined to seek the quiet enjoyment of the rights of conscience, in America. He arrived at Boston, June 5th, 1632, and in July was invested with the pastoral care of the church in Roxbury. In November following, he received John Elliot as his colleague. In 1639, he assisted Mr. Mather and Mr. Elliot, in making the New England version of the Psalms. In 1641, he was sent with Hugh Peters to England, as an agent for the province, and he never returned. He was settled at Gateshead, but was ejected in 1660, and died in the same year. He published a short story of the rise, reign, and ruin of the antinomians, familists, and libertines, that infected the churches of New England, 4to. 1644 ; 2d ed. 1692 ; an answer to W. R.'s narration of the opinions and practices of the New England churches, vindicating those godly and orthodoxical churches from more than one hundred imputations, &c. 1644.

With others he wrote the perfect pharisee under monkish holiness, against the quakers, 1654."

Allen's Biog. and Hist. Dictionary.

For specimens of his poetry, see selections from the Bay Psalm Book.

REV. RICHARD MATHER.

Mr. Mather was born in Lancashire, England, in 1596. At the age of fifteen, he became a teacher at Toxteth, near Liverpool. At the age of twenty-two, he was admitted as a student at Oxford ; but in a few months he left, was ordained by the bishop of Chester, and became the minister of Toxteth. Here he remained, abundant in labor, until 1633, when he was silenced for non-conformity, but was soon restored, and suspended again in 1634. In May, 1635, eagerly pursued by the English emissaries, he embarked at Bristol, and arrived at Boston, New England, on the 17th day of August. In just one year, he was settled over the church in Dorchester, where he spent his remaining days. He died the death of the righteous, April 22d, 1669.

Mr. Mather wrote much, and wrote well. In 1640, he assisted Mr. Elliot and Mr. Welde in making the New England version of the psalms. The Platform of Church Discipline, published at

Cambridge, in 1648, was written mostly by him. Besides these, he wrote many other works for which, see Allen's or Elliot's American Biography.

See specimens of poetry from the Bay Psalm Book.

We introduce here a brief notice of President Dunster, who, in connection with Mr. Lyon, revised that work, which was more used than any one of its time. We are sorry that we can say no more of Mr. Lyon.

HENRY DUNSTER.

"Henry Dunster, first president of Harvard College, was inducted into this office, August 27th, 1640. He succeeded Nathaniel Eaton, who was first master of the seminary, being chosen in 1637 or 1638, and who had been removed on account of the severity of his discipline. He was highly respected for his learning, piety, and spirit of government; but, having at length imbibed the principles of antipedobaptism, and publicly advocated them, he was induced to resign the presidentship, October 24th, 1654, and was succeeded by Mr. Chauncey. He now retired to Scituate, where he spent the remainder of his days in peace. He died on February 27th, 1659. He was a modest, humble, charitable man. By his last will, he ordered his body to be buried at Cambridge, and bequeathed legacies to the very persons who had occasioned his removal from the college. He was a great master of the oriental languages, and when a new version of the psalms had been made by Elliot, Welde, and Mather, and printed in 1640, it was put into his hands to be revised. He accordingly, with the assistance of Richard Lyon, improved the version, and brought it into that state, in which the churches of New England used it for many subsequent years."

Allen's Biog. and Hist. Dict.

For poetry, see BAY PSALMS REVISED.

EXPERIENCE MAYHEW.

" Experience Mayhew, minister on Martha's Vineyard, the eldest son of the Rev. John Mayhew, pastor of the same church, was born January 27th, 1673. In March, 1694, about five years after the death of his father, he began to preach to the Indians, taking the oversight of five or six of their assemblies. The Indian language had been familiar to him from infancy, and he was employed by the commissioners of the society for propagating the gospel in New England, to make a new version of the Psalms and of John, which work he execu-

ted with great accuracy, in 1709. He died
November 29th, 1758, aged eighty-five."

Allen's Biog. and Hist. Dict.

COTTON MATHER, D. D., F. R. S., &c. &c.

Few men have gained a more desirable reputation than this eminent scholar and Christian. He
was born at Boston, February 12th, 1663. His
youth was remarkable for piety and usefulness.
At the early age of fifteen, he was graduated at
Harvard College ; and even then, he had distinguished himself as a scholar. At the age of seven-
teen, he united with his father's church ; and at
twenty-one, was ordained as colleague with his
father, over the North Church in Boston. In this
office he spent his life, seeking the good of his
fellow men.

Dr. Mather was remarkable for his learning —
his industry — his expansive benevolence, and his
devoted piety. Perhaps no man of his day, had
read and retained more of the history, literature
and science of our own, and foreign countries.
His habits were the very economy of time. So
saving was he, that he placed the words " BE
SHORT," in capitals, over the door of his study, for
every visiter to read. Every morning he arranged
the duties of the day, and always devised some

method of doing good to some one ; and then his untiring industry saw it executed. His piety was that active principle, which stimulated him to seek more the good of others than his own. In his devotion he was regular and severe ; often fasting and keeping vigils. As a minister, he was devoted to his calling, and exemplary beyond the reach of impious calumny ; and his energy and faithfulness were abundantly blessed.

Dr. Mather was the most voluminous writer in the colonies. His writings are peculiar in their style, and valuable for their veracity and point, in matters of history. His publications amounted in all to *three hundred and eighty-two ;* and several of these were large works, though most were sermons and small pamphlets. Many have condemned his writings, as being full of bigotry and superstition. As regards his bigotry, it should only receive the name of firm adherence to his religious belief; and his superstition, was no more than all men at that day, both in the colonies and in England, were found to possess. He lived a life of devoted piety, and died February 13th, 1728, in the full assurance of a happy immortality.

For poetry, see PSALTERIUM AMERICANUM.

REV. JOHN BARNARD.

This eminent and justly celebrated man, was
born at Boston, Mass., November 6th, 1681.
Like most of those who have shone in the church,
he was blessed with pious parents, who had a special care over his early education.   He graduated
at Harvard College, in 1700, aged nineteen years.
During the early part of his college course, the
death of two young friends, caused him to think of
his own danger, while living thoughtless, and un-
prepared to exchange worlds.   These impressions,
though short, were soon followed by others, that
were lasting as life.   Two years after he left college, he joined the church under the charge of Dr.
Increase Mather, and during the same year began
to preach.

In 1707, he was appointed by Governor Dudley
one of the chaplains to attend the army against
Port Royal.   In 1709, he sailed for Barbadoes and
London.   In the latter place, he became acquainted with some of the famous dissenting ministers, and also received several advantageous
offers to settle there.   But these he refused,
choosing rather to return to his own native
land.   His reputation, while in England, was
truly great.

In 1714, May 23d, he preached the dedication sermon of the "New North Church," in Boston, which had been built expressly for him ; but though, at this time, he was expecting soon to be ordained, another person was chosen, and became pastor of the church. At this movement, Mr. Barnard was greatly displeased. But the Lord had work for him in another place.

In 1716, July 18th, he was ordained as colleague with the Rev. Mr. Cheever, then pastor of the church at Marblehead. In this relation, after his settlement, he remained in great harmony with Mr. Cheever, until that good man's death. Seldom do we find a man either so long, or so useful in the ministry — a public preacher *sixty-eight* years ; and *fifty-four*, a settled pastor over the same people.

Mr. Barnard was a man of great influence, both in church and state. In his own parish, he was constantly laboring for the good of his people ; for their temporal as well as their spiritual concerns. It was he, that first taught the people of Marblehead that source of profit, which has since been to them so important ; " the mystery of the fish trade."

Among the clergy of his day, he was famous for his learning, character and piety ; and his very great age, and worth of character, gave him a patriarch's sway.

"His form was remarkably erect; and he never bent, even under the imfirmities of eighty and eight years. His countenance was grand, his mien majestic, and there was dignity in his whole deportment. His presence restrained the imprudence and folly of youth, and when the aged saw him they stood up."

He was kind-hearted and benevolent; seeking to do good. In his charities, he was often silent, that the poor might rather return thanks to God, than to him. He was a great friend to education; and generally supported *two poor boys* at school; thus training others to do good.

Mr. Barnard was an humble Christian. In his last sickness, he weeping said; "My very soul bleeds when I remember my sins; but I trust I have sincerely repented, and that God will accept me for Christ's sake. His righteousness is my only dependence."

He died January 24th, 1770, in the eighty-ninth year of his age.

The following Psalms are given as a specimen of Mr. Barnard's versification.

PSALM I.   FIRST BOOK.

Thrice blest the man, who ne'er thinks fit
To walk as wicked men advise ;
To stand in sinner's Way, nor sit
With those who God, and Man, despise.

2. Whose pious soul directs his Way
By sacred Writ his sweet Delight
Thro' all the Labours of the Day ;
And meditates thereon by Night.

3. As planted Trees by Rivers Sides
Yield timely fruit a vast Encrease ;
So in first Verdure he abides
And God his Handy work will bless.

4. But those that spurn at sacred Laws,
Shall no such Favor with him find ;
For God will blast them, and their cause,
And whirl as chaff before the Wind.

5. However in the Judgment Day
The Wicked shall not stand the Light ;
Mix with the righteous shall not they
Nor any formal Hypocrite.

6. The Lord who now with pleasure views,
Will then applaud the just man's Way ;
But who his Name and Word abuse,
Shall feel his Wrath and melt away.

PSALM CXXXIV.

Lo : all ye Servants of the Lord,
Who nightly stand and wait,
Attending in his sacred House,
Jehovah celebrate.

2. Bless ye the Lord, lift up your Hands
Within his holy Place
The Lord, who Heaven and Earth hath made,
Thee out of Sion bless.

THOMAS PRINCE.

Thomas, son of Samuel Prince, of Sandwich, was born May 15th, 1687. In the autumn of 1707, he was graduated at Harvard College ; and having finished his professional studies, he sailed for England, in 1709. There he remained, preaching at Combs, in Suffolk, for some years, and was earnestly requested to remain ; but his attachment to his native land, induced him to refuse their solicitations, and to return to his friends and his home. Here, in colleague with Dr. Sewell, he became the pastor of the Old South Church, in Boston, July, 1717 ; and in this situation he remained until his death, October 22d, 1758.

Mr. Prince's literary character and works were great. Few men of his day, held a more enviable distinction.   Dr. Chauncey — and no man was better capable of judging — placed him second in learning only to Dr. Cotton Mather. He possessed a fine native genius, which he improved by diligent study, and polished by extensive acquaintance and intercourse with mankind.

His literary writings were important. While yet a member of College, he began collecting historical matter, relating to the civil and religious history of New England, and continued this work until his death. These manuscripts, with a valuable collection of books, were left to the church of which he was pastor. The books are still preserved by the Massachusetts Historical Society; but the manuscripts were destroyed by the British while they occupied Boston. He published many occasional sermons; but his two principal works, were his chronological history of New England, in 1736, and the Bay Psalm Book, rewritten, in 1758.

In private life, he was polite, amiable, and truly exemplary. As a Christian, he was meek, humble, and submissive; ever ready to forgive injuries and return good for evil. He was an eminent preacher, and inculcated the doctrines and duties of Christianity, as one who felt and practised them. When Mr. Whitfield visited Boston, Mr. Prince gave him a warm reception, assisted him in his work, and was ever an ardent friend to the revival of pure, evangelical religion. His was a life of usefulness and piety; and at his death, he enjoyed the peaceful consolations of an unwavering hope of a blessed immortality.

SPECIMENS OF PRINCE'S PSALMS.

Psalm I.

O Blessed man who walks not in
    The counsel of ill [1] men.
Nor stands within the sinner's way
    nor scoffer's [2] seat sets in.

2. But on JEHOVAH'S written law
    he places his delight;
   And in his law he meditates
    with pleasure day and night.

3. For he is like a goodly tree
    to rivers planted near;
  Which timely yields its fruit whose leaf
    shall ever green appear
  And all he does shall prosper still. [3]

[1] Ill, rather than wicked, seems more suitable for the lowest step of the treble and beautiful gradation here observed by the Learned.

[2] The Hebrew signifies scoffers; and so the Chaldee, Syriack and Arabick; i. e., such as scoff at the religion inspired by God, or at those who practice it.

[3] i. e., continually, as is plainly implied, to comport with the sense of the preceding part of the verse.

4. Th' ungodly are not so ;
   But like the chaff which by the wind
   is driven to and fro.

5. Therefore in judgment shall not stand
   such as ungodly are,
   Nor in the assembly of the just
   shall sinful men appear.

6. Because the way of righteous men
   the LORD approves and knows ;
   Whereas the way of evil men
   to sure destruction goes.

PSALM XXIII.

1. The LORD himself my shepherd is,
   want therefore shall not I ;
2. He in the folds [1] of tender grass
   soft makes me down to lie ;
   He leads me to the waters still :
3. Restore my soul does He :
   In paths of righteousness He will
   for his name sake lead me.
4. Tho' in death's gloomy vale I walk,
   yet I will fear no ill :
   For thou art with me, and thy rod
   and staff me comfort will.
5. Thou hast for me a table spread
   in presence of my foes ;
   Thou dost my head with oil anoint
   and my cup overflows.

[1] i. e., Enclosures for flocks of sheep.

6. Goodness and mercy all my days
   shall surely follow me
   And in the LORD'S house I shall dwell
   as long as days [1] shall be.

REV. ABIJAH DAVIS.

The following notice of Mr. Davis, was prepared
for the author by Judge Foster, of Millville, N. J.

" The Rev. Abijah Davis was born in the town-
ship of Deerfield, Cumberland County, N. J.,
A. D. 1763. His father, Arthur Davis, was a respectable farmer, and a deacon in the Deerfield
church. Abijah was the youngest of five brothers.
He became a member of the church where his
father belonged, at the age of about sixteen years.
At twenty-one, he married, and received from his
father a small farm, which he soon sold, and commenced his education in the college of Philadelphia, with the determination of becoming a minister of the gospel. After leaving the college, he
completed his theological studies with the Rev.
Robert Smith, of Pequa, Pa. ; was licensed by the
Philadelphia presbytery, and soon after settled at
Cold Spring, Cape May, about the year 1790. At
this place he continued to labor, until the year
1800, when he removed to Millville, and there re

---

[1] So the Hebrew and all the ancient versions.

mained until his death, in August, 1817, in the fifty-fourth year of his age.

" He was acknowledged by his brethren to be a man of strong mind, and orthodox in sentiment. In conversation, he was generally reserved, and somewhat given to melancholy. His most pleasing theme seemed to be, the *scripture prophecies*, on which subject he preached several sermons that were well approved."

Mr. Davis's principal literary work, was his version of the psalms.[1] " He was not sixteen years of age, when he formed the resolution, that at forty he would begin " the version of the psalms; and " when the time of life came, he without delay set about the work." He was engaged upon this work ten years; ten years of lost labor, unless it was for his own personal good. The work had Watts for its pattern; and some parts he varied and amplified, drawing one stanza of that admirable work into two. With slight alteration, whole psalms are copied; and *lines*, verbatim, without number. It is not a little strange, as Watts's version must have been well known in the community, and as

[1] The work had the following title: "An American Version of the Psalms of David: suited to the state of the Church in the present age of the world. By Abijah Davis, Minister of the Gospel at Millville, New Jersey."

Mr. Davis copied from him so freely, that he has not even mentioned him in his preface.   Indeed, he calls his work " a new song ; " and further : " In executing this work, the plan was to give a free translation of the Psalms, making them the ground work of the new song, preserving the leading ideas and metaphors, but varying the expression to suit the circumstances of the church in this present age of the world. . . . . It is enough for me, therefore, and it ought to satisfy every unprejudiced Christian, if in this work, I have kept as near as I could to the inspired model, without running into a jingle of words."

We will here give two or three specimens of his work ; and we are sorry that we cannot give at least one, that is purely his own.   But we cannot. The whole work is made from Watts.

The first we select, is the 146th psalm.   This is a fair specimen of the style in which he has treated many of Watts's best composures.

Psalm 146.

1. I'll praise my Maker with my breath,
   And when my voice is lost in death,
      Praise shall my nobler powers employ ;
   My days of praise shall ne'er be past,
   While life and thought and being last
      In yonder world of heavenly joy.

2. Why should I make a man my trust?
   Princes must die and turn to dust,
      Vain is the power of kings to save;
   Their breath departs, and in a day,
   Their thoughts forever pass away,
      And perish with them in the grave.

3. Happy the man whose hopes rely
   On Israel's God; he made the sky,
      And earth and seas, with all their train;
   The Lord is glorious in his deeds,
   He saves th' opprest, the poor he feeds,
      And none shall find his promise vain.

4. The Lord to sight restores the blind;
   The Lord supports the sinking mind;
      He soothes the saint when bowed with grief;
   He sets the prisoner loose, the exiled,
   The widow and the friendless child,
      Look up to God and find relief.

5. He loves his saints, he knows them well,
   But turns the wicked down to hell,
      Thy God, O Zion, ever reigns;
   Let men of every tongue and age,
   In this exalted work engage,
      Praise him in everlesting strains.

6. I'll praise him while he lends me breath,
   And when my voice is lost in death,
      Praise shall my nobler powers employ;
   My days of praise shall ne'er be past,
   While life and thought and being last,
      In yonder world of heavenly joy.

The following psalm is probably as far removed from a servile imitation, as any one we have noticed in the work.

PSALM 41.

1. Blest is the man whose tender breast,
    Has for the suffering mourner felt,
    And while his hand relieves th' opprest,
    He feels his soul with pity melt.

2. His heart contrives for their relief,
    More good than thousands could perform,
    This man in times of general grief,
    Shall find a shelter from the storm.

3. The Lord shall keep his soul alive,
    Long shall he live the blest of earth,
    And like a plant celestial thrive,
    Amid the pestilence and dearth.

4. When sick, the Lord shall stir his bed,
    And make the hard affliction soft,
    Shall raise and cheer his drooping head,
    Or bear his willing soul aloft.

In 1785, Joel Barlow published his revised edition of Watts's Psalms, in which he supplied several that Watts had omitted; and added several original hymns. As this was recommended by the

16

General Association of Connecticut, it was used quite extensively.

In 1799, a work was published, entitled, " Hymns composed on various subjects, by James Hart, Elizabethtown, N. J.   We are not acquainted with this work; nor do we know how much, or whether it was ever used.

In 1800, President Dwight, revised and published Watts's Psalms; to which he added thirty-three of his own composition.   This work was widely circulated.

Since the year 1800, there have been several writers of psalms and hymns; so many, that we are unable even to give a complete list.   Among these works are : " The Book of Psalms : Translated into English verse.   By George Burgess, A. M.   New York, 1840 ; " and " Specimens of an Improved Metrical Version of the Psalms of David.   Intended for the use of the Presbyterian church in Australia and New Zealand.   By John Dunmore Lang, D. D.   Philadelphia, 1840.

INDEX.

Accomplished Singer, 105.
Admonition to the Reader, 21.
Ainsworth, Rev. Henry, 220.
" " " Version, 13.
American Psalmists, 219.
Anecdote of Charles I., 60.

Bad Singing, 147.
Barnard, Rev. John, 237.
Barnard, Rev. J., Psalms, 157.
Bay Psalm Book, 19, 30, 50.
" " " Poetry of, 22.
" " " Improved, 25.
Bay Psalm Book Improved, Poetry of, 27.
Bay Psalm Book, Republished in Scotland, 26.
Bay Psalm Book, first used at Salem, 53.
Bay Psalm Book, first used at Ipswich, 53.
Bay Psalm Book, first used at Plymouth, 54.
Bay Psalm Book Revised, 158.
Bayley's Book, 164.
Billings's First Book, 166.
Bromfield, Edward, Jr., 152.

Cases of Conscience, 87.
Chauncey, Rev. N. 215.
" " Sermon, 123.
Choirs, origin of, 179
Church Discipline, extract, 79.
Clergy, Puritan, 19.

Clerical Influence, 142.
Controversy among Dissenters, 34.
Cotton, Rev. John, 202.
" " " Tract, 35.

Danforth, Rev. John, 214.
" " Samuel, 215.
Davis, Rev. Abijah, 245.
Different opinions concerning singing, 33.
Directions for setting the Psalm, 58.
Dunster, President H., 20, 233.
Dwight and Wightman's Essays, 122.

Edwards on Revivals, 138.
Elliot, John, 20, 221.
" " Indian Version, 55.

First American Organ, 152.
" Singing Schools, 139.
Flagg's Book, 161.

Hedge's Sermon, 190.

Indian Psalms, 55.
" Singing, 56.
Influence of Music upon Religion, 90.

Lining out the Psalm, 184.
" " " " discontinued, 199.

List of books, 170.
Luther, 10.
Lyon's Anthem Book, 159.

Mather, Cotton, 235.
"   "   extract, 79.
"   Rev. R., 20, 232.
Mayhew, Rev. E., 234.
Manner of Singing, 78.
Metrical Psalmody, 10.
Music a College Study, 50, 142.
Music first printed, 56.
"   not cultivated, 82.
"   Improved, 137.
"   held sacred, 144.
"   in use, 145.
Musical directions, 58.
"   tracts, 143.

New England Courant, extract, 89.
New England Psalm Singer, 166.
New Tunes, 113.

Origin of Metrical Psalmody, 10.
Origin of Choirs, 179.
Opposition to the Bay Psalms, 33.

Pacificatory Letter, 114.
Prejudice in Matters of Religion, 112.
Prince, Rev. Thomas, 12, 241.
Puritan Manual, 11.
"   Clergy, 19.
"   Psalmody, 48.
"   Custom, 186.
Poetry from Ainsworth, 14.
Psalmists, 219.
Psalterium Americanum, 68.

Ravenscroft's Collection, 52.
Remarks upon the Bay Psalms, 30.
Regular Singing, 90.
Reverence for Music, 77.

Reform and Reformers, 85.
"   where begun, 142.
Reformers, 202, 216.

Secomb's Sermon, 150.
Singing, 113.
"   Schools, 103, 139.
"   in Indian Churches, 56.
Shepard, Rev. Mr., 20.
Specimens from Ainsworth, 15.
Specimens from Bay Psalms, 22.
Specimens from Bay Psalms Improved, 27.
Specimens from Barnard, 240.
"   "   Davis, 247.
"   "   Indian Poetry, 55.
Specimens from Prince, 243.
"   "   Psalterium Americanum, 70.
Specimens from Sternhold and Hopkins, 61.
Sternhold and Hopkins's version, 60.
Stoddard, Rev. Solomon, 213.
Symmes, Rev. Thomas, 211.
"   Essay, 91.

Tate and Brady, 156.
Tedious Singing, 149.
Thacher, Rev. Peter, 214.
Thomas's History of Printing, 48.
Tufts's Singing Books, 65.
Tunes metamorphosed, 148.

Urania, or Lyon's Anthem Book, 159.

Walter's Singing Book, 74.
"   Introduction, 145.
Watts's Psalms, 154.
"   Extract, 187.
Welde, Rev. Mr. 20, 231.
Wightman's Essay, 122.

TESTIMONIALS.

Boston, December, 1845.

Mr. George Hood,

Dear Sir — I hope you will proceed to publish your "History of Music in New England, some parts of which, in manuscript, you some time since submitted to my inspection, and, from the very cursory view of it I then had, I thought it would be a work of some general interest, and to many readers indeed very acceptable. It would afford, I think, not only to the musical, but to the religious community, both interest and instruction, and as a mere historical tract, could not fail to engage the attention of the public.

Your obedient servant,

Nahum Mitchell.

Boston, December, 1845.

Mr. George Hood,

Dear Sir — I have read your History of Music in New England with great pleasure. In it are brought together many facts in relation to the early psalmody of New

England, which must be alike new and interesting to the present generation. I can most cordially and unreservedly recommend the work, as well worthy the attention of all who feel an interest in the cause of church music, or who reverence the character of the Pilgrim Fathers. I sincerely think it deserves, and hope it may receive an extensive patronage.

Very truly yours,
LOWELL MASON.

BOSTON, December 22d, 1845.
MESSRS. WILKINS, CARTER & CO.

Gentlemen — I have read with much satisfaction Mr. Hood's little work, entitled "History of Music in New England." It furnishes a brief, though at the same time a vivid sketch of the state and gradual progress of church music during the last century. Considered in the light of a mere history, it is highly interesting and useful. Its intrinsic value, however, consists in its being a medium to us of many excellent admonitions and teachings of great and good men of a former generation, on the uses and abuses of church music. In this point of view the work can scarcely be overestimated. GEORGE J. WEBB.

BOSTON, December, 1845.

MR. GEORGE HOOD,

Dear Sir — Having examined the proof sheets of " The History of Music in New England," it is with much pleasure that I commend it to the notice of all interested in music. No work has heretofore existed, from which a correct idea of the condition of music in this country, even at the commencement of the present century, could be obtained; but in this work we have a minute history, back to the time of the landing of the pilgrims.

I can hardly express the interest I have felt in perusing it. Those especially who have to do with church music, will find its contents not only interesting, but highly instructive.

I am, &c.

A. N. Johnson.